A COMPENDIUM
OF KISSES

LANA CITRON

HARLEQUIN®

A Compendium of Kisses

ISBN-13: 978-0-373-89242-6

© 2010 by Lana Citron

Library of Congress Cataloging-in-Publication Data
Citron, Lana, 1969—
A Compendium of Kisses / Lana Citron. p. cm.
ISBN 978-0-373-89242-6 (hardcover)
1. Kissing. I. Title.
GT2640.C57 2011
394--dc22   2010027403

www.eHarlequin.com

Printed in the U.S.A.

CONTENTS

BIBLIOGRAPHY

PREFACE

POSTHUMOUS apologies to Voltaire whose preface to his *Philosophical Dictionary* I have appropriated for my own needs, not through laziness but as prefaces go this one is the quintessence of prefaces, tripping up the reader before they have even flicked forward to page one. I bow down to his witty charm and would kiss his quill; such sentiments rendered and so daringly expressed. Reading it I felt I had stumbled upon some holy text, and it whet my appetite…moreover it made me laugh aloud. Of course, this *A Compendium of Kisses* is no philosophical work, but Voltaire's instructions on how one should read and interpret his work are exactly how I believe this book may be best enjoyed.

So, to Voltaire…

66 This book does not demand continuous reading; but at whatever place one opens it, one will find matter for reflection. The most useful books are those of which readers themselves compose half; they extend the thoughts of which the germ is presented to them; they correct what seems defective to them, and they fortify by their reflections what seems to them weak.

It is only really by enlightened people that this book can be read; ~~the ordinary man~~ *the heartless man* is not made for such knowledge; ~~philosophy~~ *philematology (the art or study of kissing)* will never be his lot. Those who say that there are truths which must be hidden from the ~~people~~ *unfeeling,* need not be alarmed; the ~~people~~ *callous* do not read; they work six days of the week, and on the seventh go to the inn. In a word, ~~philosophical~~ *philematological* works are made only for

~~philosophers~~ *philematologists (those who study kisses)* and every honest man must try to be a ~~philosopher~~ *philematologist* without pluming himself on being one.

This ~~alphabet~~ *compendium* is extracted from the most estimable works which are not commonly within the reach of the many; and if the author does not always mention the sources of ~~his~~ *her* information, as being well enough known to the learned, ~~he~~ *she* must not be ~~suspected of wishing to take the credit for other people's work~~ *accused of plagiarism* because ~~he himself~~ *she herself* preserves anonymity, according to this word of the Gospel: 'Let not thy left hand know what thy right hand doeth.' **"**

In the beginning was the word…

A Riddle

I am just two and two, I am warm, I am cold,
And the parent of numbers that cannot be told;
I am lawful, unlawful—a duty, a fault:
I am often sold dear, well for nothing when bought;
An extraordinary boon, and a matter of course,
And yielded with pleasure when taken by force.

BY COWPER[1]

The Language of Love

Kiss /kis/ v. & n. v. 1. to touch with the lips, esp. as a sign of love, affection, greeting, or reverence. 2. to express (greeting or farewell) in this way. 3. absol. (of two persons) touch each other's lips in this way. 4. to (also absol.) (of a pool ball, etc., in motion) lightly touch (another ball). n. 1. a touch with the lips in kissing. 2. the slight impact when one pool ball etc. lightly touches another. 3. a small sweetmeat of a piece of confectionery. *Kiss and tell* recount one's sexual exploits. *Kiss a person's arse* coarse slang, act obsequiously toward a person. *Kiss away*

---

1 The above riddle was originally published in *The Gentleman's Magazine.* A correspondent responded with the following answer:
    A riddle by Cowper
    Made me swear like a trooper;
    But my anger, alas! was in vain;
    For, remembering the bliss
    Of beauty's soft Kiss,
    I now long for such riddles again.
The Literature of Kissing by C. C. Bombaugh. p 373

remove (tears etc.) by kissing. *Kiss the dust* submit abjectly; be overthrown. *Kiss goodbye to* colloq., accept the loss of. *Kiss the ground* prostrate oneself as a token of homage. *Kiss off* esp. N. Amer. slang, 1. dismiss, get rid of. 2. go away, die. *Kiss the rod* accept chastisement submissively. *Kissable* adj. [Old English cyssan, from Germanic].

Kisser /kiser/ n. 1. a person who kisses. 2. (orig. boxing) slang, the mouth; the face.

Kissy /kisi/ adj. colloq., given to kissing (not the kissy type).

Oscular /oskjuler/ adj. 1. of or relating to the mouth. 2. of or relating to kissing. [Latin *osculum* "mouth, kiss," diminutive of *os* "mouth"].

Osculate /oskyuhlayt/ v. tr. 1. mathematics: (of a curve or surface) have contact of at least the second order with; have two branches with a common tangent, with each branch extending in both directions of the tangent. 2. v. intr. & tr. Joc. Kiss *osculant* adj., *osculation* n., *osculatory* adj.[2]

> "So, the next time you do some osculating, remember a kiss is not just kiss, it's some kind of psychological compulsion. A sigh, however, is just a sigh."
>
> *A Kiss is Never Just a Kiss,* Morning Edition, National Public Radio, Jan 26, 1993.

Philematology—the art or study of kissing.
Philematologist—one who studies kisses.
Philemaphobia or Philematophobia—a fear of kissing.

---

2 *The Concise Oxford Dictionary,* 9th Edition.

Kiss (v.)—Etymology of the word

O.E. cyssan "to kiss," from P.Gmc. *kussijanan (cf. O.S. kussian, O.N. kyssa, O.Fris. kessa, Ger. küssen), from *kuss-, probably ultimately imitative of the sound. The O.E. noun was coss, which became M.E. cuss, but this yielded to kiss, from the verb. There appears to be no common I.E. root word for kiss, though suggestions of a common ku- sound may be found in the Gmc. root and Gk. kynein "to kiss," Hittite kuwash-anzi "they kiss," Skt. cumbati "he kisses."

Some languages make a distinction between the kiss of affection and that of erotic love (cf. L. saviari "erotic kiss," vs. osculum, lit. "little mouth"). Fr. embrasser "kiss," but lit. "embrace," came about in the seventeenth century when the older word baiser (from L. basiare) acquired an obscene connotation. Kiss of death (1948) is in ref. to Judas's kiss in Gethsemane (Matt. xxvi.48–50).[3]

In the Dictionary of Osculation, which has never yet been completed, are found some definitions:

Buss—a kiss.

Rebus—to kiss again.

Pluribus—to kiss all around.

Syllabus—to kiss the hand instead of the lips.

Blunderbus—to kiss the wrong person,
                    sometimes unexpectedly pleasant.

Omnibus—to kiss promiscuously.

Erebus—to kiss in the dark.

Incubus—to kiss someone you don't like.

Harquebus—to kiss with a loud smack.[4]

---

3 www.etymonline.com
4 "Sweet Kisses: Poetical and Practical Ideas About Osculation."

MORSE CODE

BRAILLE

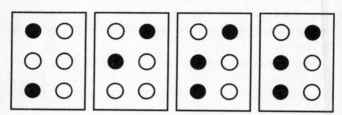

SIGN LANGUAGE

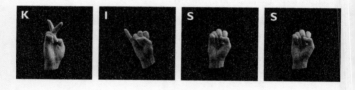

TEXT KISSES

Numerical value: 5477; also text kiss = lips.

E-MOTICONS FOR KISS

:* –kiss

:* ~ –kiss with a tongue

6

ORIGINS OF THE USE OF *X* AS A KISS

The use of the letter *X* as a symbol of affection can be traced back to when the illiterate would sign contracts with an *X* in place of a signature. Marked in the presence of witnesses, it was followed by a kiss upon the *X* to further convey sincerity. Others believe the *X*, the twenty-second letter of the Greek alphabet or Chi symbol, represents Christ or the first letter of his name and is a variation of the Christian cross. The *X* was also the ancient Paleo Hebrew letter Tav, and was a symbol of the Seal of Hashem (God) and it represented truth, completeness and perfection. In his work on the history of sex, Rabbi Brasch traces the *X* symbol for a kiss to the sign for two mouths kissing: >-<. Over time, *X* has become the universal symbol for the kiss and is also an onomatopoeic.

S.W.A.L.K.

S.W.A.L.K. is an acronym usually seen on the letters of a courting couple. It means Sealed With A Loving Kiss and is one of several acronyms that seemingly originated during the Second World War. A variant is S.W.A.K., Sealed With A Kiss. One misconception is that S.W.A.L.K. stands for Soldiers Will Always Love (the) King. Another acronym used is C.Y.K. or Consider Yourself Kissed. It was the custom in Spain to end formal letters with "QBSM," *que besa su mano,* "who kisses your hand," or "QBSP," *que besa su pies,* "who kisses your feet."

SLANG FOR KISSING

Smooch, smacker, snog, peck, "hit and miss," or "heavenly bliss," tooting bec, pec (Cockney rhyming slang), buss, canoodle, exchange spit, face time (do), Frenchy, French kiss, give one the tongue, give a tonsillectomy, give (one) some sugar, goo it, do a fade-out, first-base gab, goober, gather lip rouge, give lip, hang a goober, honey, cooler, kissaroo, kisseltoe, lip-lock, lip salute, lollygag, love peck, M.K.A. (major kiss action), mack, make kissy face, make licky face, make out, make smack lips, mow, muckle on, mug, muzzle, neck, necking, make a pass, osculate, perk, P.D.A. (public display of affection), park, pash, pass secrets, perch, plant a big one, plant a burner, plant a kissy poo, plant a smacker, play kissy, play kissy poo, play kissy face, play mouth music, play smacky lips, porch peck, rub smackers, snack smooch, smash mouth traction, frenching, spit swapping, tongue talk, hot tonguing, swapping spit, tongue to tongue, lip-sushi, sweety smooch, tongue wrestling, maraichinage, taste bud dinner, tongue tumble, jowl sucking, taste bud thirst, tonsil diving, tonsil hockey, poof, pucker up, scoop, soul kiss, taste bud projectile, tonsil swabbing, spin cycle, tongue dancing, box tonsils, tonsil swallowing, spit sampling, swab the tonsils, tonsil sandwich, tonsil boxing, hickeys bubble gum, heck bite, heck-lace, hickey hoover, strawberry-kiss, kiss bite, love bite, vac-attack, monkey bite, purple heart shag-tags, suckers prospecting, fool around, submarine race, giraffing, smooching, smoodge, smooch, smoush, spark, zoom in, give a hot-house suck face, grazing, turtle-necking, go into a huddle, lip push-ups, lip-mingling, tickling tonsils, making out, moon-tanning, tongue trekking, mugging, attend parkology, molar mashing, tongue wrestling, neck-fest, catching monk mug, muzzle, whoopie, warm up, chew face, petting, party nuzzling, explore the waists, play post office, petology fling, woo, snout, friction.

Kissing in Different Tongues

AFRIKAANS	KISS (N.) *Soen*
ALBANIAN	KISS (N.) *puthja*
ARABIC	KISS (N.) ةلبق ,تالفاح ,ليبقت KISS (V.) لبقُي ,هسوب ,ق لب
CATALAN	KISS (N.) *Petó*
CHINESE	KISS (N.) 吻 KISS (V.) 吻，接吻 (TRADITIONAL)
CROATIAN	KISS (N.) *ljubljenje, poljubac* KISS (V.) *poljubiti*
CZECH	KISS (N.) *polibek, pusa, pusinka* KISS (V.) *hubickovat, libat, polibit*
DANISH	KISS (N.) *kys* KISS (V.) *kysse*
DUTCH	KISS (N.) *buis, haringbuis, kukkel, kus,* *kusje, lik, smak, smok, zoen* KISS (V.) *aflebberen, aflikken, elkaar kussen,* *elkaar zoenen, kussen, zoenen*
FINNISH	KISS (N.) *Sitä* KISS (V.) *on sitä*

ESTONIAN	KISS (N.) *suudlus* KISS (V.) *armastama, armatsema, suudlema, suudlus*
FRENCH	KISS (N.) *baiser, bise, bisou* KISS (V.) *baiser, donner un baiser, embrasser, s'embrasser*
GALACIAN	KISS (N.) *Bico*
GERMAN	KISS (N.) *Kuss, Kuß, Küßchen* KISS (V.) *knutschen, küssen, pousseiren, schmusen, sich küssen*
HAUSA	KISS (N.) *Sumba* KISS (V.) *da sumba*
HAITIAN CREOLE	KISS (N.) *Bo*
HUNGARIAN	KISS (N.) *csók* KISS (V.) *csókol, csókolózik*
ICELANDIC	KISS (N.) *koss* KISS (V.) *kyssa*
INDONESIAN	KISS (N.) *ciuman* KISS (V.) *mencium*
IRISH	KISS (N.) *póg*
ITALIAN	KISS (N.) *bacetto, bacino, bacio, spazzolata* KISS (V.) *baciare, lambire, sbaciucchaire*

LATVIAN	KISS (N.) *skúpsts* KISS (V.) *skúpstít, skúpstíties*
LITHUANIAN	KISS (N.) *bucinys* KISS (V.) *buciuoti, buciuotis*
MALAY	KISS (N.) *Ciuman*
MALTESE	KISS (N.) *Bus*
MAORI	KISS (N.) *Kihi Ungutu*
NORWEGIAN	KISS (N.) *kyss* KISS (V.) *kysse*
POLISH	KISS (N.) *pocałunek* KISS (V.) *całowac*
PORTUGUESE	KISS (N.) *beijo* KISS (V.) *beijar*
ROMANIAN	KISS (N.) *gurã, sãrut, sãrutare* KISS (V.) *pupa, a sãruta*
SERBIAN	KISS (N.) *celov, lxublxenxe, poljubac* KISS (V.) *celivati, poljubiti,*
SLOVAK	KISS (N.) *bozk* KISS (V.) *pobozka*
SLOVENIAN	KISS (N.) *poljub* KISS (V.) *polijubiti, poljubljati se*

SPANISH	KISS (N.) *besico, beso, buz, ósculo, roce* KISS (V.) *besar, besarse*
SUOMI	KISS (N.) *pusu, suudelma, suukko* KISS (V.) *suudella*
SWEDISH	KISS (N.) *flyktig kyss, kyss, lätt kyss* KISS (V.) *kyssa, småhångla*
TURKISH	KISS (N.) *buse, öpme, öpücük, öpüs* KISS (V.) *öpmek, öpüsmek*
URDU	KISS (N.) پایر KISS (V.) پایر س ے
VIETNAMESE	KISS (N.) *hôn, nu hôn* KISS (V.) *hôn*
YIDDISH	KISS (N.) *kusch* KISS (V.) *kuschn*

I

THE ANATOMY OF A KISS

THE KISS is a most deceptive gesture. Seemingly simplistic, it is a highly complex action. Indeed, depending on the depth of passion, a kiss can ignite a plethora of emotional, sensual and physical reactions, from the meeting of lips to the dilation of one's pupils and pounding of one's heart. There may be heat beneath one's collar, perhaps even an erotic tingling. What other gesture engages all the senses: touch, taste, smell, sight and sound? This pressing of lips upon another's can ultimately involve every muscle in one's body, from the mouth to all the facial muscles, the neck, back, shoulders, the arms in which to hold each other and the legs with which to entwine.

THE PHYSICAL NATURE OF A KISS

It has taken mankind 2000 years finally to determine the anatomy of a kiss, otherwise defined as the "anatomical juxta-position of two *orbicularis oris* muscles in a state of contraction."[1] The scientific term given to kissing is *osculation* from the Latin word *osculum,* "mouth" or "kiss."

In the early 1990s, a team of scientists at University College of London, led by Professor Gus McGrouther, revealed that in order to pucker, one requires the use of all 34 facial muscles, along with 112 postural muscles which are drawn together in an action similar to a drawstring purse being pulled tight.

---

1 Dr. Henry Gibbons

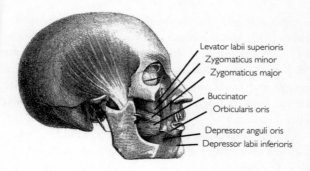

Levator labii superioris
Zygomaticus minor
Zygomaticus major

Buccinator
Orbicularis oris

Depressor anguli oris
Depressor labii inferioris

THE INSTRUMENTS OF KISSING

"How did it happen that their lips came together?"
Victor Hugo

THE LIPS

The *orbicularis oris* muscles or lips are made of muscle fibers interspersed with elastic tissues and copiously supplied with nerves. Structurally, the skin of the lips falls between the moist mucus membrane lining the mouth and body skin. As such, the lips are one of the most sensitive areas of the body.

The upward movement of one's top lip engages muscles known as the *zygomaticus major, zygomaticus minor* and *levator labii superioris*. The lower lip and corners of one's mouth are pulled downward by the *depressor labii inferioris* and *depressor anguli oris* muscles.

THE TONGUE

An openmouthed kiss involving the tongue increases the intensity of the kiss experience. Similar to the lips, the tongue is full of sensory receptors. Its interlacing muscles, the *gioglossus, styloglossus, palatoglossus* and *hyoglossus,* are used to move this versatile and flexible organ. It has a broad range of motion—one can shorten, lengthen, twist and move the tongue in very many directions.

Culturally speaking, tongues are best kept hidden. A tongue stuck out is perceived as an affront. If placed on the tip of the lips it is considered a lascivious come-on, and to lick one's lips is a sign of excited anticipation.

SALIVA

Saliva is the mucus that wets the inside of the mouth. It is filled with microscopic bacteria (single-cell organisms) that enter from air, food and dirty hands. It is estimated between ten million and one billion colonies (groups of bacteria) are swapped with each kiss. Reassuringly, saliva also contains antibacterial chemicals that kill most bacteria before the germs are exchanged in a kiss.

BABY KISSES

A human embryo has a distinct mouth, set of lips and an upper and lower jaw by the time it is six weeks old or a mere half an inch long. It is about this time that the tongue and vocal cords begin to form. By the third month, the fetus is able to open and close its mouth and press its lips together.

TONGUE KISSING
OR FRENCH KISSES

Passionate, open-mouth kissing with tongues has never been confined to boundaries, space or time. Popularly known as the French kiss, this national adjective has various sexual connotations, and its synonymy is thought to date back to the height of Anglo-French enmity in 1730–1820. Thus we have a spate of allusions (though many now redundant), hence *French lessons* translating as services offered by a prostitute, *French prints* signifying pornographic prints and to be "Frenchified" as having syphilis.

Later on, the French Revolution was a term adopted by the U.S. Gay liberation movement. *French letter* came to be used as an euphemism for a condom, which in turn the French call a *capote anglaise.*[2]

A possible predecessor of the term *tongue kiss* is the *maraichinage,* popularized by the residents of Pays de Mont in Brittany. The Maraichins practiced a deep-tonguing kiss, whereby each partner explored the other's mouth in a tongue battle simulating genital penetration.

> *"A soft lip, would tempt you
> to an eternity of kissing."*
> Ben Johnson

---

2 Brigid McConville, and John Shearlaw, *The Slanguage of Sex.*

LIP SHAPES

The ideal lip shape is a matter of taste and time. Lips styles follow sociocultural mores and socioeconomic factors. This is most evident by taking a glance at the leading ladies of the silver screen whose lip shapes dictate what is presently in vogue.

Back in the days of black-and-white movies, at a time of prohibition and rebellion, lips in fashion were the "Cupid bow" as pursed by Clara Bow, the vampish lips of Theda Bara and the "bee-sting" as pouted by Mae Murray. Then came the war years—times of austerity, but also burgeoning female independence, and with it the straight-lipped sensuality of Greta Garbo and Marlene Dietrich. Full symmetrically styled mouths followed in the '40s, as displayed by Rita Hayworth, Joan Crawford, Bette Davis and Katherine Hepburn.

The postwar period heralded a more feminine and slinky look: think Marilyn Monroe, whose full lips preceded the more provocative pout of Brigitte Bardot, the latter a ripe symbol of '60s sexual freedom. However, as female emancipation gained ground, alongside the more overt female sexuality on show was the beautiful Audrey Hepburn, whose lips were boyish, a precursor to the androgynous look of the '90s.

These days anything goes. There is no predominant style although the plump-pillow look, as presented by the plush pouts of Beatrice Dalle, Julia Roberts and Angelina Jolie, has recently reigned supreme. There is, however, a thin line between what is considered attractive and what is not. Mick Jagger's lips are regarded as sexually potent whereas English politician Michael Portillo's large pair are often depicted as being too wet or rubbery.

n.b. Aesthetics versus Functionality

Whilst "bee-stung" lips and "Paris" lips are only a modestly priced collagen implant away, surgery does affect lip sensitivity. Note also the aesthetic value of the "trout pout" has, of late, undeniably deflated.

Lip Ethics

Although not always considered socially acceptable, the coloring of one's lips has been in practice since time immemorial. Far from being a mere frivolous beautifying exercise, it has been used to denote, among other things, status, class, profession (clowns, actresses and prostitutes[3]) and political acts of defiance.

In Western culture, the church denounced lip painting as altering God's most precious gift and in 1770, the English Parliament passed a law declaring that women who seduced men into matrimony through use of lip and cheek paints could have their marriages annulled, as well as face witchcraft charges. Specifically, the legislation declared:

> All women of whatever age, rank, profession or degree, whether virgins, maids or widows, that shall, from and after such Act, impose upon, seduce and betray into matrimony any of His Majesty's subjects, by the scents, paints, cosmetic washes, artificial teeth, false hair, Spanish wool, iron stays, hoops, high-heeled shoes

---

3 Under ancient Greek law, prostitutes who appeared in public either at the wrong hours or without their designated lip paint and other makeup could be punished for improperly posing as ladies.

or bolstered hips, shall incur the penalty of the law in force against witchcraft and the like misdemeanors and [their] marriage[s], upon conviction, shall become null and void.[4]

In the early twentieth century, the suffragettes used lipstick as a sign of emancipation. Leaders such as Elizabeth Cady Stanton and Charlotte Perkins Gilman advocated the wearing of lip rouge as an emblem of women's emancipation and incorporated its use into the 1912 New York Suffragette Rally, choosing to sport a specific shade of red. "In both America and England, women publicly applied lip rouge with the express intent of appalling men. Lipstick's long proscription by social, religious, and legal male authority made it a ready symbol for female rebellion."[5]

LIP SHADES

Ingredients used to color the lips have included white lead, crushed rocks, red ochre, red dye, plant stains, wine, sheep sweat, human saliva, crocodile excrement, bear fat, mercury and arsenic pomatum, wax, ox's marrow, alkanet root, brandy, vermilion (colored mercury sulfide), hog's lard, spermaceti, almond oil, balsam, raisins, sugar, carmine, strawberry juice, beet juice, hollyhock, coal tar dyes and gold leaf.[6] The ancient Minoans used a purplish-red pigment produced from a gland in the murex shellfish; Elizabeth I used a mixture including cochineal, gum Arabic, egg white and fig milk.

---

4 Richard Corson, *Fashions in Makeup from Ancient to Modern Times.*
5 Sarah Schaffer, *Reading Our Lips: The History of Lipstick Regulation in Western Seats of Power.*
6 Ibid.

TATTOOED LIPS
–indelibly yours

A more extreme method of lip color application was tattooing. George Burchett (1872–1953) was London's leading tattooist for more than fifty years. Known as the Beauty Doctor, his clients included actresses, doctors, judges, a bishop and assorted royalty including King George V of England and the late King Frederick of Denmark. He perfected the technique of tattooing red dye into the pouting lips of young starlets. "Unhappily this treatment backfired (if the aspiring actress actually made it to Hollywood), as orthochromatic film, being sensitive to every color except red, had a nasty habit of turning her lips black."[7]

LIPSTICK

...or the "stick of love" as the actress Sarah Bernhardt named it, was officially born in 1883. Perfumers from Paris presented a lipstick made out of tallow, wax and colored castor oil, wrapped it in paper and presented it at the World Fair in Amsterdam. The paper had to be peeled back in strips every time the lipstick was used. In 1915, Maurice Levy of the Scovil Manufacturing Co. in Connecticut, realized that he could mass-produce and distribute the popular sticks of lip color by packaging them in protective metal push-up tubes. The first swivel lipstick was patented by James Bruce Mason Jr. in 1923. The case had a decorative screw head that was turned as the lipstick was depleted. In 1930, Max Factor created lip gloss to give actresses' lips a moist appearance.

---

7 Lindy Woodhead, "Stars with Scars."

THE OSCILLATING OSCULATOR

In 1939, Max Factor, Jr. created The Kissing Machine or Mechanical Osculator to test the indelibility of lipstick because workers previously employed for the purpose quickly tired of the job. Instead, rubber molds of their lips were taken and attached to a pressure gauge. Tissue paper inserted between pairs of rubberized lips calculated how many prints it took before the lipstick wore off.[8]

PHYSIOLOGICAL EFFECTS OF KISSING

A kiss can trigger a cascade of neural messages and chemicals that transmit tactile sensations, sexual excitement and even electricity (albeit only if extraordinarily lucky or sensitive). Of the twelve to thirteen cranial nerves that affect cerebral function, five are at work when we kiss. Information about temperature, taste, smell and the physical movements of the kiss, is sent to a swath of brain tissue called the somatosensory cortex. This tissue represents all tactile information in what can be described as a sensory map of the body. In that map, the lips loom disproportionately large to that of their actual size. This is because the size of each represented body region is proportional to the density of the nerve endings.

---

8   Jane Garcia, "Factoring in Beauty—A Hollywood Museum Celebrates the Artistry of a Cosmetics King."

Lipstick Kiss-Tester Spoils a Nice Job

So THAT lipstick won't come off, even when treated as above, a Hollywood Calif., make-up expert has resorted to the novel "kiss-test" machine in the foreground of the picture. Run by electricity, the oscillating osculator repeatedly presses together artificial lips of plastic—after one set has been coated with the lipstick preparation to be tested—upon a sheet of white paper. At the first sign of a visible imprint on the paper, a counter shows how many contacts the lipstick has survived. Previous experiments with live subjects showed so much variation in kissing technique and ardor that the machine was substituted.

The above article appeared in *Popular Science* in March 1940.

LANA CITRON

THE CHEMISTRY OF A KISS

"A young lady's first-love kiss has the same effect on her as being electrified. It's a great shock, but it's soon over."[9]

Upon lip-locking of an erotic nature, a flush of various hormones courses through the body. The most important ones are dopamine, oxytocin, serotonin and adrenaline. Oxytocin is a hormone connected to social bonding. It helps people develop feelings of attachment, devotion and affection for one another. Dopamine is linked to the brain's processing of emotions, such as pleasure and pain. Serotonin affects a person's mood and feeling. Adrenaline increases one's heart rate and plays a major role in the body's fight-or-flight impulses.

Or should the above be too scientific…

THE COMPOSITION OF A KISS
—as described by Samuel T. Coleridge

Cupid, if storying legend tell aright,
Once framed a rich elixir of delight.
A chalice o'er love-kindled flames he fix'd,
And in it nectar and ambrosia mix'd;
With these the magic dews, which evening brings,
Brush'd from the Idalian star by fairy wings:
Each tender pledge of sacred faith he join'd,
Each gentler pleasure of th' unspotted mind—

9   C. C. Bombaugh A.M. M.D., *The Literature of Kissing.*

Day-dreams, whose tints with sportive brightness glow,
And Hope, the blameless parasite of Woe.
The eyeless chemist heard the process rise,
The steamy chalice bubbled up in sighs;
Sweet sounds transpired, as when the enamour'd dove
Pours the soft murmuring of responsive love.
The finish'd work might Envy vainly blame,
And "Kisses" was the precious compounds name.

THE SHAPE OF A KISS

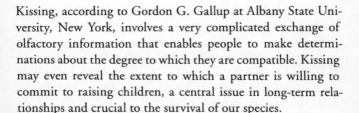

Needless to say, the shape of a kiss is "a lip tickle" (sic)! And what part of speech is a kiss? "A conjunction," of course! And have you ever considered why a kiss is like a rumor? Well, because it passes from mouth to mouth....

Moving swiftly on...

THE SCENT OF A KISS

Kissing, according to Gordon G. Gallup at Albany State University, New York, involves a very complicated exchange of olfactory information that enables people to make determinations about the degree to which they are compatible. Kissing may even reveal the extent to which a partner is willing to commit to raising children, a central issue in long-term relationships and crucial to the survival of our species.

However, whether humans sense pheromones is controversial. Unlike rats and pigs, people are not known to have a specialized pheromone detector between their nose and mouth. Nevertheless, there is sufficient evidence to suppose that pheromones do play a role in human courtship and procreation. Thus, kissing is an extremely effective way to pass them on from one person to another. Biologist Sarah Woodland of Duquesne University suggests humans are able to sense pheromones via our noses.

> *"With a taste of your lips I'm on a ride,*
> *you're toxic, I'm slipping under."*
> Britney Spears, "Toxic"

Kiss Casts

Artist Charlie Murphy has developed a unique way of capturing an everlasting kiss in which audience members of her international "Kiss-in" events are invited to participate. A quick-setting dental casting material is spooned into their mouths, and then they kiss each other, holding a pose for a minute until the cast sets. The casts are later transformed into glass trophies visualizing their internal kisses.

The Weight of a Kiss

In the aforementioned Gallup survey, it was found that attraction to a potential partner evaporated after their first kiss, if the kiss in question was deemed unsatisfactory. Such kisses had no specific flaws; they just did not "feel right."

The reason a kiss carries such weight is that it conveys subconscious information about the genetic compatibility of a prospective mate. From a Darwinian point of view, sexual selection is the key to passing on genes. Research has proven that women prefer men with immune system proteins that are different from their own. In theory, having a baby with someone with different immune proteins can lead to healthier offspring. Scientists believe that a woman may be able to smell these proteins while kissing and that what she smells may affect whether she finds her partner attractive.

In his writing, late first-century Roman epigrammatist Martial romanticized the fragrance of a kiss as "the scent of grass which a sheep has just cropped; the odour of myrtle, of the Arab spice-gatherer."

THE SOUND OF A KISS

According to C. C. Bombaugh who, heard it from a wag:[10]

> When two pairs of affectionate lips are placed together to the intent of osculation, the sound of a kiss reads something along the lines of this: *Epe-st'weep'st-e'ee!* And then the sound tapers off so softly and so musically that no letters can do it justice.

The unnamed wag, Bombaugh states, continues with a challenge:

> If anyone thinks my description imperfect, let him surpass it if he can, even with a pen made from a quill out of Cupid's wing.

Christopher Nyrop in his 1901 book *The Kiss and Its History*, explains that from a "purely phonetic point of view a kiss may be defined as an 'inspiratory bilabial' sound, which English phoneticians call the lip-click, for example, the sound made by smacking the lip."

10   C. C. Bombaugh A.M. M.D., *The Literature of Kissing.*

In *The Mechanism of Human Speech* by Wolfgang von Kempelen (Wien, 1791), kisses are divided into three sorts, according to their sound. Firstly there is the *freundschaftlich hellklatschender Herzenkuss*—an affectionate, clear ringing kiss coming from the heart. Next a more discreet, or—from an acoustic point of view—weaker kiss; and lastly, a third type designated an *ekelhafter Schmatz* or "loathsome smack."

Or as Oliver Wendell Holmes, Sr. put it in *The Professor at the Breakfast Table:* "The sound of a kiss is not so loud as that of a cannon, but its echo lasts a great deal longer."

KISS CALORIES

If one's mind is on calories whilst kissing, there can be no hope for love. However, it is known that some have a penchant for such inanities…so: the energy used in a kiss is of course, totally dependent upon one's depth of passion but a general estimate given is between 2–6 calories a minute.

THE TASTE OF A KISS

How to capture the taste of a kiss? The most fitting description is that it is sweet. During the Renaissance, popular expressions used were *bouche sucrine* and *bouche pleine de sucre et d'ambergris* (mouthful of sugar and ambergris). A Latin epigram describes it thus:

What is sweeter than mead? The dew of heaven and what is sweeter than dew? Honey from Hybla and what is sweeter than honey? Nectar. Than nectar? A kiss.[11]

BREATH

According to the Trebor Mighty Mint "Mouth Mauling Survey," nothing is guaranteed to ruin one's chances of being kissed more than bad breath. Seven out of ten people surveyed said that smelly breath was the biggest passion killer of all. The worst smells rated were smoker's breath, garlic breath, stale beer and curry. Other off-putting things included a hairy top lip (on men and women), tonsil tickling, spotty skin and flaking dandruff.

MOUSTACHES

Kate hates moustaches; so much hair
Makes every man look like a bear;
But Nellie, whom no thought could fetter
Pouts out, "the more like bears the better,
Because" (her pretty shoulders shrugging)
"Bears are such glorious chaps for hugging."[12]

11 Christopher Nyrop, *The Kiss and Its History.*
12 C. C. Bombaugh A.M. M.D., *The Literature of Kissing.*

RUNNY NOSES

...are hardly enticing either. Martial evokes the nauseous experience of having to kiss lips and faces covered with dirt, snot, ulcers and gangrene, and foul running sores. In his epigram (vii 95) Martial describes Linus as an affectionate person with a long beard and a cold nose who never misses the chance to kiss on a winter's day. "Pray put it off," Martial cries, "put it off until April!" These kissers, or "basiatores" as he called them, were the poet's *bête noire*.

> No doubt, the icicles hanging at thy dog like snout,
> The congealed snivel dangling on thy beard,
> Ranker than th' oldest goat of all the herd.
> The nastiest mouth in town I'd rather greet,
> Than with thy flowing frozen nostrils meet.
> If therefore thou hast either shame or sense,
> Till April comes no kisses more dispense.

DENTISTRY

Attending to one's breath and ensuring its sweetness is nothing new. The Romans of the imperial age sweetened their breath with myrrh. It is hardly surprising that with the advent of more effective dentistry and as halitosis diminished, the allure of the openmouthed kiss increased.

Once again, Martial has something to say on the subject in a little epigram to Posthumus.

What's this that myrrh doth still smell in thy kiss,
And that with thy no other odour is?
'Tis doubt, my Posthumus, he that doth smell
So sweetly always smells not very well.

At certain times in history in Western society, the custom of greeting one another with a kiss on the mouth was wholly acceptable and regarded as being without sexual intent. The cleaning-up of the mouth bore cultural implications for those kisses of social and ritual purpose. As the sexual connotations of a lip-on-lip kiss became more apparent, it was replaced by different words and actions less susceptible to ambiguity, for instance the handshake.

Stiff Upper Lips

In the fifteenth century, the English social kiss between men and women had been on the lips. This disappeared over time due in part to the eroticization of the kiss; the kiss on the cheeks as practiced in France was less blatantly sexual and accordingly proved more enduring. By the 1960s, societal inhibitions began to relax and the social kiss slowly returned to England.

Handy Kisses

The International Scientific Forum on Home Hygiene states that greeting someone with a kiss on the cheek is more hygienic than a handshake.

ASYMMETRICAL KISSING

It is estimated that two-thirds of people tip their heads to the right when kissing. Obviously we tilt our heads to avoid bumping noses, but scientists have wondered why it should be to the right and not the left.

Various experiments have been carried out on behavioral asymmetry, which is related to the compartmentalization of brain functions such as speech and spatial awareness. A 2006 study by naturalist Julian Greenwood in Belfast found that 77 percent of subjects tilted their heads to the right when kissing a doll, for example, an object to which there was no emotional attachment (given the subjects were adults and not little girls). Likewise 80 percent of 125 kissing couples tilted their heads to the right.

> *"Whoever named it necking*
> *was a poor judge of anatomy."*
> Groucho Marx

German psychologist Onur Gunturkun of Ruhr University, Bochum, suspects that right-tilted kissing results from a general human preference. This preference develops at the end of gestation when babies tip their heads to the right in the womb. Studies have also shown that 80 percent of mothers, whether right-handed or not, cradle their infants on their left side. Thus, a baby is more used to turning its head to the right to nurse or nuzzle. It is deduced then that most of us have learned to associate warmth and security with turning to the right. Does this necessarily mean then that a left-sided kiss is less emotional and colder?

And if cursed with innocence or inexperience, one may find the following instructions helpful:

HOW TO KISS

"People will kiss, though not one in a hundred knows how to extract bliss from lovely lips, any more than they know how to make diamonds from charcoal; yet it is easy enough. First, know whom you are going to kiss; do not jump up like a trout for a fly and smack a woman on the neck, or the ear or the corner of her forehead or on the end of her nose. The gentleman should be a little the taller; he should have a clean face, a kind eye, and a mouth full of expression. Do not kiss everybody; do not sit down to do it; stand up. Take the left hand of your lady in your right; let your hat go to—anywhere out of the way; throw the left hand gently over the shoulder of the lady and let it fall down the right side. Do not be in a hurry; draw her gently, lovingly, to your heart. Her head will fall submissively on your shoulder, and a handsome shoulder strap it makes. Do not be in a hurry. Her left hand is in your right; let there be an impression to that, not like the gripe of a vice, but a gentle clasp, full of electricity, thought and respect. Do not be in a hurry. Her head lies carelessly on your shoulder; you are heart to heart. Look down into her half-closed eyes; gentle, but manfully; press her to your bosom. Stand firm; be brave, but do not be in a hurry. Her lips are almost open; lean slightly forward with your head, not the body; take good aim; the lips meet; the eyes close; the heart opens; the soul rides the storms, troubles and sorrows of life (don't be in a hurry); heaven opens before you; the world shoots under your feet as a meteor flashes across the evening sky (don't be afraid); the heart forgets its bitterness and the art of kissing is learned! No fuss, no noise, no fluttering or squirming like that of hook-impaled worms. Kissing doesn't hurt, nor does it require an act of Congress to make it legal." [13]

So now you know....

13 C. C. Bombaugh A.M. M.D., *The Literature of Kissing.*

THE KISS OF LIFE[14]

The phrase *The Kiss of Life* was first coined in 1961 in the *Daily Mail*.[15]

In 1745, members of the Royal Society of London attended a lecture given by John Fothergill on an unusual practice that has come to be known as the Kiss of Life, by which we mean mouth-to-mouth resuscitation. Back then, it was known as "blowing back the breath."[16]

> And if you'd see, what you do much desire,
> The object of your care again respire
> Let one the mouth and either nostril close,
> While th' inflating bellows up the other blows
> The air with well-adjusted force convey
> To put the flaccid lungs again in play
> Should bellows not be found or found too late
> Let some kind soul with willing mouth inflate
> Them lightly squeeze—awhile compress the chest,
> That the excluded air may be exprest

BY WILLIAM HAWES, 1796

BLOWING BACK THE BREATH

This type of resuscitation can be traced back to the Bible, to Elijah's miraculous revival of a dead boy, upon whom he "put his mouth upon his mouth, and his eyes upon his eyes and his hands upon his hands."

It was also a practice widely used by midwives to try to revive stillborn babies, recorded as far back as the fifteenth century.

---

14 Luke Davidson, "The Kiss of Life in the 18th Century: The Fate of an Ambiguous Kiss."
15 Ibid. p. 99.
16 The Bible. 2 Kings 4:34.

THERE ARE KISSES AND THEN THERE ARE KISSES....

Fothergill was much excited by the idea of the Kiss of Life, as it would do away with the use of artificial respiration by the bellows. However, the idea failed to ignite a warm reception. Eighteenth-century doctors, though aware of its lifesaving potential, refused to adopt mouth-to-mouth resuscitation as a respectable medical practice and as such, it lapsed until James Elam and Peter Safar reintroduced the idea in the 1950s, two hundred years later.

A KISS LIKE NO OTHER—100% PC

The Kiss of Life differs from other kisses in that it is administered in crises where the recipient is usually unconscious and is the only beneficiary. It is a kiss no one is expected to take any pleasure from. It is supposed to be useful rather than gratifying or meaningful. Cultural and social boundaries do not constitute proper grounds for not performing the kiss. In matters of life and death the victim's race, sex and/or creed is of no consequence.

> *"To blow ones own breath into the lungs of another is an absurd and pernicious practice."*[17]

Fothergill had hoped the Kiss of Life would help with victims of drowning. At this time the near-drowned were hung by the heels to drain or rolled over a barrel to have the water squeezed out of their cavities. Other methods of reviving patients included warming and rubbing the body, applying brandy to the skin, taking blood, using smelling salts and intro-

---

17 B. Waterhouse, *On The Principle of Vitality.*

ducing tobacco smoke into the rectum. The latter would lead to sweating, vomiting and defecation. Added to this unpalatable picture was the general state of the victim's mouth.

CHEESY KISSES

As this was a period of bad dental health, it is no wonder mouths in portraits were kept zipped up; foul and missing teeth were the lot of most gums. What dental delights, one wonders, lay behind the Mona Lisa's smile?

Madame Vigee-Lebrun, considered the most famous female painter of the eighteenth century, bucked the millennia-old tradition of keeping one's mouth firmly closed and revealed in her 1787 self-portrait a smiling set of pearly whites.

SWEET-TOOTHED MOUTH MADNESS

A considerable increase in the consumption of sugar and chocolate had predictable effects on teeth; coffee, tobacco and gin led to halitosis. The use of mercury as a specific for syphilis caused dental staining, the loss of teeth and twice the normal levels of salivation, amounting to 3–4 pints a day. Most people believed the mouth was a contagious cavity, and that the breath spread venereal diseases. It was hardly surprising that administering the Kiss of Life was considered unseemly, gauche and a rather disgusting and disagreeable practice, if not downright foolhardy.

According to Alan Corbin, a doctor in the 1790s administered mouth-to-mouth upon a cesspool cleaner asphyxiated by the overwhelming stench in his workplace. The doctor, Monsieur Verville, "had scarcely inhaled the air that was coming from the mouth of the mortally ill man," an onlooker reported, "when he shouted 'I am a dead man!' and fell down unconscious."[18]

---

18   Luke Davidson, "The Kiss of Life in the 18th Century: The Fate of an Ambiguous Kiss."

Viral Kisses
—ever-so contagious

The Roman Emperor Tiberius (A.D. 14–37) issued a decree banning kissing because it was believed to be responsible for the spread of an unpleasant fungus disease called Pentagram, which disfigured the faces and bodies of Roman nobles.

Kissing can lead to a variety of infectious diseases....

Sick Kisses

THE KISSING DISEASE

A well-known kissing disease of the 1950s and '60s is *mononucleosis* or *mono,* the cause of extreme fatigue and depression; even liver disease. The infection is literally swallowed during kissing, allowing the microbe to enter the body. It is estimated that up to 95 percent of adults have been infected at some time in their lives. Unsurprisingly, it proliferates where there are concentrations of young adults.

STREP THROAT

Streptococcus microbes, which can cause an array of infections, including gum disease and strep throat, preponderate by adhering to the inner surface of the cheeks and mouth, the tongue or teeth.

HEAD LICE

Beware the tangled mess of hair spread out upon a pillow or running fingers through your loved one's tresses; lice can easily jump from head to head. Itching and scratching is a sure giveaway.

TRENCH MOUTH OR GUM DISEASE

Most adults carry the bacteria that cause red inflamed gums and bone deterioration that leads to the loss of teeth—watch out for sniveling, spluttering, coughs, white tongues, un-healthy-looking gums and rotten breath.

MOUTH ULCERS

As the respiratory tract (nose, mouth and throat) is continuous, infections such as colds and flu can be carried in saliva. Some researchers even theorize that gastric ulcers may spread through kissing.

COLD SORES

In contrast to infections spread through saliva, the *herpes simplex virus* is spread through open cold sores on the lips or near the mouth. Perhaps obviously, the infection is most contagious when the sore is open and leaking fluid.

STUBBLE RASH

How many have fallen prey to this particular type of grazing, most commonly a by-product of an ardent new passion, such that we of the fairer sex with softer skin are so enamored as to allow the shredding of our chins.

HAND, FOOT AND MOUTH

Coxsackie virus is another infectious disease spread through open sores in the mouth. A common infection among toddlers, it spreads primarily via the fecal-oral route. It is common in nurseries due to the continuous changing of diapers.

But canker sores are not infectious. In contrast to cold sores and Coxsackie virus blisters, canker sores have no infectious disease origin and cannot be spread through the saliva or kissing.

THE KISSING BUG

This blood-sucking insect from the family *reduviidae* that transmit the parasite *trypanosoma cruzi* is held responsible for spreading the debilitating Chagas disease. Chagas disease is a tropical parasitic disease common in Latin America and, if left untreated, can cause serious intestinal and heart problems.

KILLER KISSES

An estimated one in ten teens carry the meningococcal bacteria, which can lead to *meningitis* (an inflammation of the brain lining) and *septicemia* (blood poisoning) both of which can be fatal. Indiscriminate kissing can quadruple the risk of catching meningitis.

AIDS

Despite the presence of HIV in saliva, it is virtually impossible to catch the HIV virus through kissing. However, the United States Center for Disease Control has reported one suspected case of transmission this way.

Despair Not...

On the plus side, the mouth has natural defenses in the form of saliva, which regularly flushes it out; and antibodies, which counteract harmful bacteria.

Futhermore, kissing stimulates the brain. It creates food for thought, produces a feel-good factor and boosts one's self-esteem. Its direct health benefits are numerous: sharing bacteria can aid one's immune system. Kissing is good for the heart, as it creates an adrenaline rush causing your heart to pump more blood around your body. It decreases blood pressure and cholesterol. Those who kiss quite frequently are less likely to suffer from stomach, bladder and blood infections.

Preventing Kissing Diseases

Put succinctly, be careful who you kiss.
Or take precautions…

THE KISSING SHIELD
—for hypochondriacs and politicians who kiss a lot of babies

U.S. Patent 5787895 (otherwise known as the Kissing Shield) is a simple, inexpensive shield formed of a thin, impervious membrane within a frame, which can be used when kissing to prevent the exchange of germs and the unsightly transfer of lipstick or other cosmetics.

HAZARDOUS KISSES

Despite the hazards of kissing, the general consensus is that kissing is good—physically, emotionally and spiritually. Its benefits are lauded in poetry, literature, film, music. The Greeks say that the kiss is the key to paradise, a preservation against every ill: *"No ill luck can betide me when she bestows on me a kiss,"* sings Colin Muset.

Its powers of revival are part of folklore. Heine declares: *"Yet could I kiss thee, O my soul, then straightaway I should be whole."*

According to the Duke of Anhalt, kissing carries life with it and even bestows the gift of eternal youth: *"If on that mouth a kiss I were bestowing, Methinks I should in sooth become immortal."* [19]

Alas, the state of immortality is an abstract conceit.

---

19 Christopher Nyrop, *The Kiss and Its History.*

THE DEATH KISS

"I sit by the form in the coffin, I kiss and kiss convulsively again the sweet old lips, the cheeks, the closed eyes in the coffin."
Walt Whitman, "As at Thy Portals Also Death"

Not to be confused with the Kiss of Death—synonymous with betrayal and vendetta—this kiss is the last tender proof of love bestowed on one we have cherished and was believed in ancient times to follow mankind to the netherworld. The death kiss is not only a mark of love, but also expresses the belief that the soul might be detained for a brief while by such a kiss. Ovid, in his *Tristia*, laments his joyless exile in Tomis, and despairs because when the hour of death approaches, his beloved wife will not be by his side to detain his fleeting spirit by her kisses mingled with tears.

> Popular belief in many places demands that the nearest relative kiss the corpse's forehead ere the coffin lid is screwed down. In certain parts it is incumbent on every one who sees a dead body to kiss it otherwise he will get no peace for the dead.[20]

Kissing a dying loved one on the lips is a commonly used literary tool. Ann Pasternak maintains that Shakespeare's characters kiss the dying on the mouth for three reasons: to revive them, to conclude the relationship in a final mingling and to help transport the soul to the afterlife.

---

20 Christopher Nyrop, *The Kiss and Its History.*

ANTHONY. *I am dying, Egypt, dying; only*
I here importune death awhile, until
Of many thousand kisses the poor last
I lay upon thy lips.

CLEOPATRA. *And welcome, welcome! Die, where thou*
hast lived; Quicken with kissing; had my lips
that power, Thus would I wear them out.

ANTHONY AND CLEOPATRA IV.13

ROMEO. *Eyes look your last! Arms, take your last embrace!*
and lips, O you, The doors of breath seal with a
righteous kiss

JULIET. *Drink all and leave no friendly drop,*
To help me after?—I will kiss thy lips
Haply, some poison yet doth hang on them,
To make me die with a restorative.

ROMEO AND JULIET V.3

OTHELLO. *I kissed thee ere I killed thee,—no way but this,*
Kissing my self to die upon a kiss.

OTHELLO V.2

"ADDORMENTARSI NEL BACIO DEL SIGNORE"

The Italian expression "to fall asleep in the Lord's kiss" takes the idea of dying to a higher level. What better way to tempt one to the next world than to liken death to a comforting, homecoming kiss of affection bestowed by God?

"He who takes His child in His arms, kisses it, and carries it away from earth to brighter and more blissful spheres."[21] Amen and kiss, kiss.

Life's autumnal blossoms fall,
And earth's brown clinging lips impress
The long cold kiss that waits us all.[22]

Gravestone Kisses

Lost life by stab in falling on ink eraser evading
six young women trying to give him birthday
kisses in office Metropolitian Life Building.

The above relates to the saddest of fates of George S. Millitt. Employed in the Department of Applications of the Metropolitan Life Insurance Company, he was stabbed in the heart by the sharp ink eraser (a knife used for scraping mistakes) he carried in his pocket when six female stenographers came to give him a birthday kiss.

Son of a widow, he had been employed merely two months when the incident occurred. On learning it was his fifteenth birthday the office girls teased him that they would kiss him once for every year he had lived. "He laughingly declared that not a girl should get near him. However when the end of the day came the girls made a rush. They tried to hem him in and he tried to break their line. Suddenly he reeled and fell, crying, 'I'm stabbed.'"[23] The boy died before he reached the hospital without recovering consciousness.

---

21 Ibid. p. 96.
22 C. C. Bombaugh A.M. M.D., *The Literature of Kissing.*
23 "Stabbed to Death in Office Frolic."

II
THE NATURE AND GEOGRAPHY OF A KISS

THE NATURE OF A KISS

UNIVERSAL KISSES

*"Look at these people! They suck each other!
They eat each other's saliva and dirt!"*
—Tsonga people of Southern Africa
on the European practice of kissing.[24]

SNIFFS AND KISSES

Charles Darwin noted that in various parts of the world kissing[25] "is replaced by the rubbing of noses." Often referred to as a Malay kiss, Darwin likens it to a handshake and unsurprisingly the word for kiss and salute in many Malay tribes are one and the same. A common assumption is that rubbing noses is for the Inuit the equivalent of kissing. Indeed, early explorers of the Arctic called it the Eskimo kiss.

Yet *kiss* is not an accurate comparison, as the Inuit were not just rubbing noses, they were smelling each other's cheeks. Practiced among the Chinese Yakuts and various Mongolian peoples, and even the Lapps of Northern Finland, Paul d'Enjoy described it thus: "The nose is pressed on the cheek, a nasal inspiration follows, during which the eyelids are lowered, lastly there is a smacking of the lips."[26]

---

24 Henri A. Junod, *The Life of a South African Tribe.*
25 Alfred Ernest Crawley, *Studies of Savages and Sex.*
26 Ibid.

The olfactory kiss as named by Havelock Ellis was well known in Africa. "In the Gambia when a man salutes a woman he takes her hand and places it to his nose, twice smelling the back of it. Among the Jekris of the Niger coast mothers rub their babies with their cheeks or mouths, but they do not kiss them, nor do lovers kiss, though they squeeze, cuddle, and embrace. Among the Swahilis a smell kiss exists, and very young boys are taught to raise their clothes before women visitors, who thereupon playfully smell the penis; the child who does this is said to 'give tobacco.'"[27] In societies which have demurred from kissing, people have licked, sucked, rubbed, nipped, blown on or patted their sexual partner's face.

"Well, I Never...!" Kisses

Havelock Ellis, in accordance with his Darwinian notion that erotic kissing was a mark of more advanced civilizations, declared that the kiss was "not usually found among rude and uncultured peoples."[28] However, modern research suggests that just about every culture on the planet kisses; 90 percent of humans kiss according to anthropologists.

Kisses in Exchange for the Potato and Tobacco

European explorers introduced the practice of kissing to many cultures across Africa, the Pacific and the Americas. In these soci-

---

27 Havelock Ellis, *Studies in the Psychology of Sex IV: Sexual Selection in Man.*
28 Ibid.

eties, where the practice of kissing seems to have played a less conspicuous part in either erotic life or ritual, kissing appears to have been deemed disgusting or distasteful, and the act of exchanging saliva revolting. Bear in mind some researchers point out that these societies may view kissing as too private to discuss with strangers. In other words, they might kiss but not talk about it. Among the Lapps, both sexes would bathe naked, but kissing was taboo.

Soulful Kisses

"Her lips suck forth my soul."
Marlowe

Some African tribes did not kiss on the mouth because the mouth was considered the portal to the soul, thus one could steal souls by kissing, or invite in germs and death. Ancient lovers apparently believed a kiss would unite their souls, because the spirit was said to be carried in one's breath.

"Soul meets soul on lovers' lips."
Percy Bysshe Shelley, *Prometheus Unbound.*

Nineteenth-century French naturalist and explorer Alfred Grandidier noted "the invisible air which is continually being breathed through the lips is to savages, not only as with us, a sign of life but it is also an emanation of the soul—its perfume, as they themselves say—and, when they mingle and suck in each other's breath and odour they think they are actually mingling souls."

Soul-sucking has always been a favorite allegory of the poetic vanguard. Alfred Lord Tennyson wrote "Once he drew with one long kiss my whole soul thro' My lips, as sunlight drinketh dew." And Robert Browning in *A Toccata of Galuppi's* conjectured, "What of soul was left, I wonder, when the kissing had to stop?"

VAMPIRE KISSES

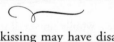

The vampire's kiss is the reverse of the traditional soul-touching kiss—instead of feeding the soul, the kiss of the vampire sucks away life, allows evil to penetrate and destroys moral fiber. A vampire's kiss signifies moral death—it steals the soul and the peace of heavenly rest. One either dies outright or joins the legions of undead preying on the living, destroying decency. A watered-down vampire becomes the independent vamp. Yet, in societies where kissing was regarded with disdain, perhaps it was not only the soul that had to be protected.

CURTAILING KISSES

It is understood that kissing may have disappeared in some societies for cultural reasons. Its prohibition was common among many African tribes, particularly among those with facial mutilations. "The insertions of rings and other mutilating objects in female lips and the widespread practices of clitorectomy and infibulations may be," argues Adrienne Blue, "an attempt to subjugate female sexuality." In the travel book *Savage Africa* (c. 1862), William Winwood Reade recalls the horror that seized a young African woman when he kissed her.

P.D.A. OR
"PUBLIC DISPLAYS OF AFFECTION"

To this day public kissing is regarded as indecent in many parts of the world due to cultural customs, social class and/or religious belief. In 1990, the Beijing-based *Workers' Daily* advised its readers that, "The invasive Europeans brought the kissing custom to China, but it is regarded as a vulgar practice which is all too suggestive of cannibalism."[29]

> *"Lord, I wonder what fool it was*
> *that first invented kissing?"*
> Jonathan Swift

EVOLUTIONARY KISSES

CHICKEN OR EGG KISSES

Kissing may not be a wholly universal practice, so how then to decide if it is an innate trait, like language and laughter, or a learned behavior? Are we genetically predisposed to pucker up or is it a gesture that caught on as a passionate virus?

There is no conclusive consensus among scientists, though most agree that the motions of sucking and kissing are inter-related. Sucking, an innate trait, uses the same muscles and

---

29 Joshua Foer, "The Kiss of Life."

movements as kissing, so it is believed to be an open instinct, where learning joins the dots left by genetics. Our ability to suckle is easily transformed to kissing.

THE UN-KISSED

As sentient beings, there is no doubt we need affection. We need to be touched and loved. Babies are genetically programmed to become attached to someone, an inclination known as "monotropy."

In a grim twentieth-century experiment it was discovered that infants raised in orphanages, fed on schedule yet hardly ever kissed, picked up or held, often lost interest in living and died of a disease known as *infant marasmus*, literally meaning "wasting away."[30]

BABEL KISSES

According to the thirteenth-century *Chronicles of Salimbene*, the German Emperor Frederick II wanted to discover what language children would speak if no one ever spoke to them and thus discern "what language would have been imparted unto Adam and Eve by God." He chose several newborns and instructed the nurses to feed them, but provide no cuddling or talking. Again all of the babies died, "for the children could not live without clappings of the hands, and gestures, and gladness of countenance, and blandishments."

---

30 Adrienne Blue, *On Kissing*.

LANA CITRON

REGURGITATED KISSES

Certain anthropologists have suggested that mouth kissing is a relic gesture, the evolutionary origins of the "kiss-motion" stemming from the mouth-to-mouth feeding that occurred be-tween mother and baby in an age before baby food. Chimpanzees feed in this manner as do a variety of many cubs and pups, thus it has been argued our hominid ancestors most probably did, too. Pressing out-turned lips against the lips of offspring may then have developed as a way to comfort hungry children when food was scarce and in time, to express love and affection. Humans might then have taken these proto-parental kisses down other roads until we came up with the more passionate varieties we have today.[31]

There remain certain tribes that continue to kiss-feed their children. The childcare habits of the warlike Yanomami of Venezuela are quite foreign to those of a Westerner: parents "don't hesitate to kiss their baby sons' penises or suck them to put the child in a better mood," apparently a trick well known by governesses in Europe and America in the nineteenth century.[32]

GREEDY KISSES

Lovers the world over pass food and drink to one another between kisses. Indeed, kissing itself as a form of insatiable hunger is a well-versed poetic allegory. The theme of Roman writer Catullus's famous poem, in which he demands hundreds, then thousands of kisses from his lover, is surely one of gluttonous love:

31 Chip Walter, "Affairs of the Lips, Why We Kiss."
32 Adrienne Blue, *On Kissing*.

Kiss me now a
thousand times &
now a hundred
more & then a
hundred & a
thousand more again
till with so many
hundred thousand
kisses you & I
shall both lose count

Byron wishes "womankind had but one rosy mouth to kiss them all at once from north to south."

Certainly, there is a return to the sensuous primary experience of tasting another person when indulging in romantic kissing. When we kiss we devour the subject by caressing it. In a sense we eat it, but sustain its presence. As Adam Philips entertainingly puts it: "If in a crude psychoanalytic interpretation, kissing could be described as aim-inhibited eating, we should also consider the more nonsensical option that eating can also be as Freud will imply aim-inhibited kissing."[33]

FREUDIAN KISSES
—all about the boob

"No one who has seen a baby sinking back satiated from the breast and falling asleep with flushed cheeks and a blissful smile can escape the reflection that this picture persists as a prototype of the expression of sexual satisfaction in later life," wrote Freud in *Three Essays on Sexuality* (1905).

---

33 Adam Philips, *On Kissing Tickling and Being Bored.*

For Freud, kissing was a subconscious return to suckling at the mother's breast. This experience, the use of the tongue and lips and aroma of body and skin, the touch on the face, suggests that every kiss from infancy on reverberates with deeply felt echoes of attachment, pleasure, feeling good and gives kissing its emotional power.[34]

However there is a significant difference between a child ingesting milk and two adults kissing. In infancy the flow is one way—the child will eventually be satiated whereas the adult's hunger can only increase; hunger in this case being desire.

Other commentators have noted the sexual correlation; that the lips bear a striking resemblance to the labia, and that women across the world go to great lengths to enhance their lips in size and color to simulate the appearance of sexual arousal, like animals in heat.

OR PERHAPS... A FREUDIAN SLIP OF TONGUE

Not every one agrees with Freud's analysis. In *Human Ethology* by Irenäus Eibl-Eibesfeldt, it is argued that "Freud read the direction of evolution erroneously. Patterns of caressing primarily evolved in the service of parental care (nurturing the child) and only secondarily became incorporated in the preparatory of courtship behaviour."

"What did that mean, to kiss?
You put your face up like that to say goodnight
and then his mother put her face down.

---

34 Leonore Tiefer, *The Kiss —A 50th Anniversary Lecture.*

That was to kiss. His mother put her lips on his cheek;
her lips were soft and they wetted his cheek;
and they made a tiny little noise: kiss.
Why did people do that with their two faces?"
James Joyce, *Portrait of the Artist as a Young Man* (1916)

Bipedal Kisses
—upright standing

The vertical posture of humans and the emotional power of eye-to-eye contact, further increases the intimacy of the gesture.

Animal Kisses

Animal life provides numerous analogies: there is the bill and coo of birds, the antennal play of insects. Indeed many mammals lick each other's snouts. Nevertheless we should not anthropomorphize and view these gestures as anything but the act of grooming. What we see as kissing is more likely to be the smelling of scent glands located on the face or in the mouth. Still, when animals touch each other in this way, they are often showing signs of trust or developing social bonds. Chimpanzees even give platonic pecks on the lips. Only humans and our lascivious primate cousins, the bonobos, engage in openmouthed tongue kissing, but the fact that other primates kiss does lend credence to the idea that the desire to kiss is instinctive.

MONKEY LOVE

Bonobos are celebrated as peace-loving, matriarchal and sexually liberated primates. Considered the closest relative of humans, it is claimed that "every bonobo—female, male, infant, high or low status—seeks and responds to kisses."[35]

In his article "Tension Regulation and Non-reproductive Functions of Sex in Captive Bonobos," bonobo expert Frans de Waal reported on the diverse sexual habits of these primates, which, he discovered, were not solely related to reproduction and had more in common with human sexual practices. Their sex life was varied and pleasure-seeking, as well as used to resolve conflict and tension. He also saw forty-three instances of kissing, some involving "extensive tongue-to-tongue contact." However his findings have come under recent scrutiny by fellow primatologist, Gottfried Hohmann, who has been studying them in the wild. "Tongue-kissing apes? You can't come up with a better story."[36]

INTERSPECIES CANOODLING

"Auugh! I've been kissed by a dog!
I have dog germs!
Get some hot water! Get some disinfectant!
Get some iodine!"
Lucy Van Pelt in *Peanuts* by Charles Schulz

35 Ibid. The Kinsey Report.
36 Ian Parker, "Our Far Flung Correspondents Swingers."

We humans are an indiscriminate lot and readily shower affection on all types of living beings, and as any animal lover will argue, it is not a one-sided affair. The famous American zoologist Dian Fossey, who undertook an extensive study of gorilla groups, describes in her journals how the female gorilla reacted to her after an absence of three years: "She lay down beside me and embraced me. GOD she did remember."

ROBOTIC KISSES

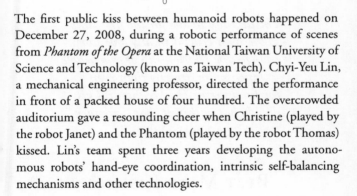

The first public kiss between humanoid robots happened on December 27, 2008, during a robotic performance of scenes from *Phantom of the Opera* at the National Taiwan University of Science and Technology (known as Taiwan Tech). Chyi-Yeu Lin, a mechanical engineering professor, directed the performance in front of a packed house of four hundred. The overcrowded auditorium gave a resounding cheer when Christine (played by the robot Janet) and the Phantom (played by the robot Thomas) kissed. Lin's team spent three years developing the autonomous robots' hand-eye coordination, intrinsic self-balancing mechanisms and other technologies.

ON FROGGIE KISSES

A popular literary interspecies coupling is that of the maiden and frog. In matters of romance the fairer sex are warned that they must kiss many of these amphibians in search of a prince. It is unclear from where this motif originates, but the meaning behind it is generally accepted as true.

MISS PIGGY: *Kermit, do you notice that every time we have a beautiful girl on the show, you forget about me?*

KERMIT: *Uh, yeah, well, we could have a seal act on the show, and I might forget about you.*

MISS PIGGY: *He tries so desperately to hide his love for me.*[37]

THE EVOLUTIONARY PSYCHOLOGY OF KISSING

*"The decision to kiss for the first time
is the most crucial in any love story.
It changes the relationship of two people
much more strongly than even
the final surrender; because this kiss
already has within it that surrender."*
Emil Ludwig

BEST MATE KISSING

As previously noted, from a Darwinian perspective, sexual selection is the key to passing on your genes. For humans, choice of mate often involves falling in love. Thus, kissing plays an important role in the courtship/mating ritual. In a study published in September 2007, Gordon Gallup surveyed 1,041

---

37 *The Muppet Show.* August 10, 1976 (Season 1, Episode 15).

college undergraduates of both sexes about romantic kissing.[38] Their findings suggested significant differences between genders with regard to the importance of the kiss.

VENUS KISSES

"Women still remember the first kiss after men have forgotten the last."
Gourmont

Women place more importance than men on kissing as a mate-assessment device and as a means of initiating, maintaining and monitoring the status of their relationship with a long-term partner—natural, given their greater parental investment and limited reproductive potential. Females also have a better sense of smell and taste compared to males, which increases during ovulation, putting them in a better position to assess potential mates. For females, an important physical feature in deciding whether to kiss someone was the appearance of their teeth. Females also felt that a male who was a bad kisser was less desirable as a potential mate.

---

38   Gordon G. Gallup, Jr., Marissa A. Harrison, and Susan M. Hughes, "Sex Differences in Romantic Kissing Among College Students: An Evolutionary Perspective."

Mars Kisses

*"A man snatches the first kiss, pleads for the second,
demands the third, takes the fourth,
accepts the fifth and endures all the rest."*
Helen Rowland

In contrast and as predicted, men place less importance on kissing and appear to use kissing to increase the likelihood of having sex. Men also placed more importance on facial attractiveness, the attractiveness of the person's body and their weight. Males showed a greater preference for wetter kisses. It is possible that kissing styles that maximize salivary exchange provide subtle information about a female's reproductive status, since saliva and breath odor change across the menstrual cycle. However it may just be that men regard increased moisture when kissing as a sign of greater sexual receptivity on the part of their partner. Overall, the data shows that males feel kissing should lead to sex more often than do females.

*"Alcohol is like love. The first kiss is magic,
the second is intimate, the third is routine.
After that you take the girl's clothes off."*
Raymond Chandler

Post-Coital Kisses

Both sexes agreed that females are more likely to initiate kissing after sexual intercourse. This supports other findings in showing that men tend toward a hasty post-sex departure, distancing themselves physically and emotionally to reduce the likelihood of bonding and investment in short-term mating partners. Furthermore, both men and women report that the ability to kiss well contributes to making someone a good lover.

It Started with a Kiss

"A kiss is the upper persuasion for a lower invasion."
Unattributed

Kissing is considered by both sexes an activity that can increase sexual arousal and receptivity, and may facilitate the occurrence of sexual intercourse. Thirteenth-century troubadour Robert de Blois put it more poetically in his manual on the behavior of women *Le Chastiement des Dames*: "The kiss leads to other things and when it so pleases a woman that she wants and desires it there is no doubt about the rest."

Voltaire concurs and warns: "Behold the danger: there is one nerve…which goes from the mouth to the heart, and thence lower down, with such delicate industry has nature prepared everything! The little glands of the lips, their spongy tissue, their velvety paps, the fine skin, ticklish, gives them an exquisite and voluptuous sensation, which is not without analogy with a still more hidden and still more sensitive part. Modesty may suffer from a lengthily savoured kiss between two Pietists of eighteen."[39]

---

39   Voltaire, *Philosophical Dictionary.*

KISSING AND INTIMACY

Our good friend Nyrop writes that a romantic kiss surpasses all other earthly joys in sublimity, a sentiment with which I whole-heartedly agree. Does not the heart near explode with antic-ipation in the lead-up to one's first "love" kiss? Undoubtedly intimate is this meeting of lips, as tongue laps tongue and a sensory symphony awakens. A most reciprocal action, there is no distinction between give-and-take, as lover devours lover. "In Kissing do you render or receive?" asks Cressida in *Troilus and Cressida*. Adrienne Blue describes the erotic kiss as a mutual penetration of the sensory oasis of the face. Indeed, many regard romantic kissing as a more intimate act than sex. It is no accident that those love stories, which have attained the power of myth often use the kiss instead of coitus to represent sexual love and intimacy. In contrast, when sex is transacted for money, for example, in prostitution and porn, the kiss is traditionally absent (although pornography specifically targeted at a female audience does include kissing and is also a feature of gay porn). Prostitutes often refuse to kiss clientele because kissing is synonymous with a genuine desire and love for the other person. Their refusal to kiss clients is thought to be an emotionally distancing technique.

In a scene from Milan Kundera's collection *Laughable Loves*, a couple play the Hitchhiking Game. Pretending they are strangers who have picked each other up, he rebuffs her when she tries to kiss him, saying, "I only kiss women I love."

Kama Sutra Kisses

*"Anything may take place at any time
for love does not care for time or order."*
Kama Sutra

Much is made of kissing in this ancient Indian text. Considered the primary Sanskrit work on human sexuality, the Kama Sutra devotes an entire chapter to it. In the case of a young maiden, Vatsyayana wrote there are three sorts of kisses:

When a girl only touches the mouth of her lover with her own, but does not herself do anything, it is called the *nominal kiss*.

When a girl, setting aside bashfulness, wishes to touch the lip that is pressed into her mouth (the lower lip, not the upper one), it is called the *throbbing kiss*.

When a girl touches her lover's lip with her tongue, and having shut her eyes, places her hands on those of her lover, it is called the *touching kiss*.

Also described are the *straight kiss, the bent kiss, the turned kiss, the pressed kiss, the kiss of the upper lip* and the *clasping kiss*. Regarding the latter, a woman only takes this kind of kiss from a man who has no moustache. This sacred text pays due diligence to the erotic kiss, the practice of and intent within. A *kiss that kindles love* is when a woman looks at the face of her lover while he is asleep and kisses it to show her intention or desire. When a lover coming home late at night kisses his beloved, asleep in bed, in order to show her his desire, it is called a *kiss that awakens*. When a woman is shampooing her lover's body, places her face on his thigh (as if she was sleepy) so as to inflame his passion, and kisses his thigh or great toe, it is called a *demonstrative kiss* and so on and so forth.

The importance of kissing in lovemaking is cited in *The Perfumed Garden* by Sheikh Nefzawi. Japanese pillow books also tell lovers to enjoy the taste of each other's saliva, but Sheikh Nefzawi has the last word: "a kiss is one of the most potent stimulants that a man or woman can indulge in…and is more intoxicating than strong wine."

COLD COMFORT KISSES

In contrast Alex Comfort's *Joy of Sex* devotes a mere page to kissing…although the cover uses an image of a kissing couple as an euphemism for what lies between the pages. "A good mouth kiss," we are told, "should leave its recipient breathless but not asphyxiated."

TONGUE-IN-CHEEK KISSES

Voltaire writes, "the kiss designed by nature for the mouth has often been prostituted to membranes which do not seem made for this usage. One knows of what the Templars were accused…"[40]

---

40 Voltaire, *Philosophical Dictionary.*

Lipless Kisses

"Fan Kisses" were an eighteenth-century method of inviting a kiss. The fan, when pressed to the lips, indicated the anticipation of a kiss. The pressure of the fan on the mouth would often indicate the level of sincerity and passion involved.[41]

Butterfly kisses or eyelash kisses all aflutter can be used to stimulate sensitive parts of the body such as nipples or upper lip and philtrum. Not to be confused with the Glasgow Kiss, Glaswegian slang for a head butt.

> *"A kiss with a fist is better than none."*
> Florence and the Machine

Latin Love

The ancient Romans had three kinds of kisses: *oscula,* meaning friendly kisses; *basia,* kisses of love; and *suavia,* passionate kisses. *Basia coniugibus, sed et oscula dantur amicis, suavia lascivis miscantur grata labellis.* "*Basia* are given to spouses, but *oscula* to friends; Let delicious *suavia* be mingled on lascivious lips."

---

41 Colin Blakemore, and Sheila Jennett, "Kiss."

Breathless on Kisses
—a dizzying array

What the Kama Sutra highlights is that there is no such thing as a straightforward kiss. Consider the infinite variety of ways in which a kiss can be delivered, and upon what and where it can be planted. This flipperty gibbet of a gesture evades classification and for the purposes of this section we will stick to those kisses of a bonding nature, and no better kiss to begin with than the first lips with which we are usually met.

BONDING KISSES—
from the Affectionate to the Erotic

"There, There" Kisses

"The mother's first kiss teaches the child love."
Guiseppe Mazzini

From the moment we are born we are welcomed into the world with kisses, and during our first years as we struggle to our senses and feet, we are plastered with "kiss it better" platitudes and "there, there" affirmations of comfort and security.

Pat it, kiss it,
Pat it, kiss it,
Stroke it, bless it:
Three days sunshine, three days rain
Little hand all well again

Maternal Kisses

Proust wrote a hundred pages obsessing over a maternal kiss. In *Remembrance of Things Past*, the seven-year-old remembers his mother kissing him good-night:

> "My sole consolation when I went upstairs for the night, was that Mamma would come in and kiss me after I was in bed. The moment in which I heard her climb the stairs, and then heard the whisper of her blue muslin dress, from which hung tiny tassels of plaited straw, rustling along the double-doored corridor, was for me a moment of the utmost pain because it heralded the moment which was to follow it, when she would have left me and gone down stairs again… When she had bent her loving face down over my bed and held it out to me like a host for an act of peace-giving communion in which her lips might imbue real presence and with it the power to sleep."

And continuing on the same theme,

> "I would often ask her," says Farjeon, "being of an inquisitive turn of mind, Mother, what have you got for dinner today?" "Bread, Cheese and Kisses," she would reply merrily. Then I knew that one of our favourite dishes was sure to be on the table and I rejoiced accordingly. And to this day, Bread and Cheese and Kisses bears for me in its simple utterance a scared and beautiful meaning. It means contentment; it means cheerfulness; it means the exercise of sweet works and gentle thought; it means Home!"[42]

---

42 C. C. Bombaugh A.M. M.D., *The Literature of Kissing*.

Nursery Rhyme Kisses

A kiss when I wake in the morning
A kiss when I go to bed
A kiss when I burn my fingers
A kiss when I bump my head

A kiss when my bath is over
A kiss when my bath begins
My mamma is full of kisses
As full as nurse is of pins

—*The Literature of Kissing*

A father's kiss, though different, is of no less importance. Homer describes the moment when Hector takes leave of his wife and child to return to the battlefield in a most touching manner:

Thus having spoke, the illustrious chief of Troy
Stretched his fond arms to clasp the lovely boy.
The babe clung crying to his nurse's breast,
Scared at the dazzling helm and nodding crest;
With secret pleasure each fond parent smiled
And Hector hastened to relieve his child,
The glittering terrors from his brow unbound,
And placed the beaming helmet on the ground,
Then kissed the child, and, lifting high in air,
Thus to the gods preferred a father's prayer.

—*Iliad* p. vi

On a more domestic front, Virgil writes:

His cares are eased with intervals of bliss:
His little children climbing for a kiss,
Welcomes their father's late return at night;
His faithful bed is crowned with chaste delight.

—*Georgics II* p. 523

Familial Kisses

It is customary, even in places where public displays of affection are scorned and erotic kisses deemed immoral (unless within the confines of marriage), for family groups to kiss one another.

In ancient times, there was a so-called *jus osculu*, which allowed all of a woman's relations to kiss her. There are several curious stories linked to the origin regarding this law, the most common being that it allowed the kisser to divine whether or not a woman (forbidden to drink wine) had imbibed alcohol in the absence of the kisser.

However, familial kisses, it was noted, lacked a certain zing.

"To kiss one's sister is not particularly unpleasant, but it is only a bread-and-butter affair. Good, but not sweet. To kiss one's cousin is somewhat different, and gives a jam taste to the operation, particularly if she comes under the denomination dangerous. But to kiss somebody else's sister or cousin, that surpasses the other as far as ice cream and cake surpass bread and jam."[43]

Laurence Sterne called it "flesh and blood with an angel on the inside."

---

43 "Sweet Kisses." *Bruce Herald*

BIKE SHED KISSES

Now, onward to that time and place where many a first fumbling occurred, when many a surreptitious note was passed declaring an amorous intent, and one virgin set of lips was met by another. Most recall this awkward time between childhood and adulthood, indeed no matter how hard one tries to forget, some memories stain the consciousness in a fundamental manner, coloring the very fibers of our being.

Bike sheds[44] are synonymous with adolescent first kisses, closely followed by the local park,[45] and then when night falls, the school disco.[46]

Oh the sheer pain of it….

THE LOVE KISS
—or knee trembler

…you have yearned, dreamed and longed for this meeting of lips, his/hers upon yours, and with eyes dilated, heart pounding, blood rushing—a quivering mess—you raise your lips to his/hers,

---

44 Furtive fumblings behind the bike sheds have recently been outlawed in England and Wales. In the government's efforts to protect children from abuse, a law forbids under-sixteens from engaging in any sexual activity—ranging from touching to full intercourse. The scope of the act could well include kissing, although the government has assured teenagers that consensual acts have never been, nor will be, punished. "Teenage Kissing: The New Sex Crime?" By Giles Wilson, BBC News Online Magazine.

45 In the local parks in Chile, teenagers known as "Pokemones" have been scandalizing society. On a typical Friday afternoon in the capital, Santiago, hundreds gather for bouts of sexual experimentation, disregarding other park-goers. Meanwhile, in South Africa it is against the law for anyone under the age of sixteen to take part in any public displays of affection. This has led to large protests across the country by teenagers, culminating in kiss-a-thons in public.

46 In a district of Jakarta, Indonesia, hundreds of youths participate in a highly unusual annual kissing (*omed-omedan*) ritual, standing men on one side, women on the other. They nominate friends to be kissers until every member of the group has had their turn.

and the world cracks open…all is possible…you are in the moment, of the moment, momentarily lost…and found.

In the case of lovers, a kiss is everything. Socrates declares, "There is nothing which stirs up the fire of love so much as kisses."

> *"A long, long kiss, a kiss of youth and love,*
> *And beauty, all concentrating like rays*
> *Into one focus, kindled from above;*
> *Such kisses as belong to early day."*
>
> Byron

However, since time immemorial men have been warned of the subversive powers of a kiss. A common maxim declared that if trapped by love, a man faced lapsing into effeminacy.

"Do you think," said Socrates to Xenophon, "that love kisses are not venomous, because you do not see the poison? Know that a fair woman is more dangerous than scorpions."

PASSIONATE KISSES

Aghhhh…the type that afford no mercy, kisses in which to lose one's self, kisses to drown in, the quenching, burning kisses of love… The great (evidently very potent) Persian poet Hafiz wrote that his mistress was afraid "his too hot kisses will char her delicate lip."

These are kisses of a branding, bruising kind, that leave love imprints upon you. These are nibbling, biting kisses, *baciare co'denti* as the Italians have it, and a precursor of the vampire kiss.

KEEPSAKE KISSES

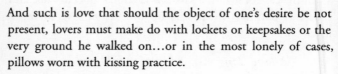

And such is love that should the object of one's desire be not present, lovers must make do with lockets or keepsakes or the very ground he walked on…or in the most lonely of cases, pillows worn with kissing practice.

And sadder still…

THE ANCIENT MAIDEN'S LAMENT

> I have a mouth for kisses
> No one to give or to take
> I have a heart in my bosom
> Beating for nobody's sake
> —*The Literature of Kissing*

STOLEN KISSES

When are kisses sweetest? When syrupticiously obtained. (!)

Roman law defined such kisses as *crimen osculationis,* kisses borne of one-sided lust and taken without permission. Punishment was dependent on proof of the perpetrator's unchaste intentions, and proportioned in severity according to the rank and status of the injured party, most severe in the case of a nun and married woman.

The French expressed it most aptly: *Un baiser n'est rien, quand le cœur est muet.* "A kiss is nothing when the heart is mute." The

Danes wrote that: "A kiss snatched by force is an egg without salt," and the Germans likened it to a corn on one's foot.

In 1837 a certain Thomas Saverland paid through the nose for his stolen kiss:

"On Tuesday, Caroline Newton was indicted for assaulting Thomas Saverland, and biting off his nose. The complainant, whose face bore incontestable evidence of the severe injury inflicted, the fleshy part of the left nostril being entirely gone, stated, that the day after Christmas-day he was in a tap-room, as were the defendant and her sister. The sister laughingly observed that she had left her young man in Birmingham, and had promised him no man should kiss her while absent. Complainant regarded the observation as a challenge, especially it being holiday time, and caught hold of her and kissed her. She took it in good part, as a joke, but defendant [her sister] became angry, and desired she might have as little of that kind of fun as he pleased. Complainant told her if she was angry he would kiss her also, and tried to do so; a scuffle ensued and they both fell to the ground. After they got up complainant went and stood by the fire, and the defendant followed and struck at him. He again closed with her, and in the scuffle he was heard to cry out, 'She has got my nose in her mouth.' When they parted he was bleeding profusely from the nose, and a portion of it, which defendant had bitten off, she was seen to spit out of her mouth upon the ground. The defendant, a fat, middle-aged woman, treated the matter with great levity, and said he had no business to kiss her sister, or attempt to kiss her, in a public house; they were not such kind of people. If she wanted to be kissed, she had a husband to kiss her, and he was a much handsomer man than defendant ever was, even before he lost his nose. The Chairman told the jury that it mattered little which way their verdict went. If they found her guilty the court would not fine her more than 1s., as the prosecutor had brought the punishment on himself. The jury, without hesitation, acquitted her. The Chairman told the prosecutor he was sorry for the loss of his nose, but if he would play with cats, he must expect to get scratched. Turning to the jury the Chairman afterwards said, 'Gentlemen, my opinion is that if a man attempts to kiss a woman against her will, she has a right to bite his nose off if she has a fancy for so doing.' 'And eat it too,' added a learned gentleman at the bar. The case caused much laughter to all except the poor complainant."[47]

"No Means Yes" Kisses

"Every girl is fond of kisses, though she may pretend to scorn them," says Nyrop and adds, "no is not always to be taken seriously. The refusal may, you know, be merely feigned—a woman's 'no' has often a piquancy about it which lovers of a somewhat more refined class set great store by."

In support he quotes first epigrammatist Martial and French poet Marot:

"While every joy I scorn but that I snatch
and me thy furies more than features catch."
Martial

---

47 *Bell's New Weekly Messenger*, April 30.

*"Mouth of coral, rare and bright, that in kissing
seems to bite, longed for mouth I pray you this,
feign deny me when you kiss."*

Marot

Kiss her gently, but be sly;
Kiss her when there's no one by:
Steal your kiss, for then tis meetest
Stolen kisses are the sweetest.[48]

It would seem that a woman is—by virtue of even having lips—if not shouting "kiss me, kiss me," then at least silently mouthing the words. Indeed, is it not a woman's right to feign restraint? A German maiden's proverb teases "I cannot bear kissing when I am not taking any part in it."

"I never give a kiss," says Prue
"To naughty man, for I abhor it."
She will not *give* a kiss, 'tis true:
She'll *take* one, though, and thank you for it.

—Anonymous, "The Difference"

A definite no is best illustrated by this wonderful put down from Bette Davis, from *Cabin in the Cotton*, 1932: "I'd love to kiss you but I just washed my hair."

Undoubtedly women are aware, too, of the witchery that dwells on their lips and the power that lies in their kiss. A power that if exerted correctly can lead to a fine old state…otherwise known as matrimony.

MAY THIS BE A WARNING TO MEN OF ALL AGES…

"The Danger Of Osculation," *West Coast Times,* January 13, 1874, New Zealand.

---

48 C. C. Bombaugh A.M. M.D., *The Literature of Kissing.*

The New York Court of Appeals has just affirmed the decision of the Brooklyn City Court in the case of Homan v. Earle. This decision practically abolishes kissing in affixing thereto the penalty of matrimony at the discretion of the kisses. To thousands of gay butterflies and pretty innocents this news will be of deep and painful interest. The story of the case is the following: A few months ago Miss Roxelana Homan brought a suit in our neighboring city for breach of promise against Mr. Alexander Earle, a prosperous merchant. Mr. Earle imagined that before Roxelana could gain her case she must make the promise appear. He denied it, and calmly "just like a man," upon the law and logic of the matter.

Miss Homan admitted there was no promise, verbal or written, but founded her claim upon the fact that Earle had frequently kissed her. While the unhappy man was congratulating himself upon his easy escape, his heart within him was turned to stone by these inconceivable words from the Bench, spoken by Judge Neilson, with measured accents and slowly flapping ears. He charged that no words were necessary to constitute an engagement. "The gleam of the eye, the conjunction of the lips," said this light of jurisprudence, "are overtures when they become frequent and protracted." The jury, always eager to do a thing which shall be at once idiotic and gallant, gave Roxelana $15,000 for the wear and tear of her lips and affections.

Of course the case was appealed, and the higher tribunal has promptly confirmed the decision of the Court below. It is therefore the law at this hour in the State of

New York that "if a bachelor kisses a spinster, said spinster may rightly claim his hand or his goods." In cases where shyness or lack of opportunity may have prevented actual osculation, the young lady has still another string to her beau; if she can show that he has ever "shined his eye" in her direction, he is her lawful spoil, according to Judge Neilson. There is positively "no protection for a bachelor except nose-bags and blind-bridles, and the ability to prove he has never left them off."

The practical results of this momentous decision are appalling. No youth who values his liberty will hereafter suffer himself to be kissed except by a lady who can show her marriage certificate, and bring proof that her husband is living. With this exception, this soothing and humanizing amusement must be confined to the domestic circle, and the young man of the future will be "doomed mere sisterly salutes to feel, insipid things, like sandwiches of veal."

"I do" Kisses or "The Overture Kiss to the Opera of Love"[49]

Some Christians hold the belief that the wedding kiss symbolizes the exchange of souls between the bride and the groom, fulfilling the scripture that "the two shall become one flesh." However the root of the tradition may be explained through an ancient Roman tradition. Much like a handshake, the Romans' exchange of a kiss was used to sign a contract. Roman Emperor Constantine declared a woman betrothed be entitled to half her intended's effects should he die before they were married.

---

49 C. C. Bombaugh A.M. M.D., *The Literature of Kissing.*

A kiss after a wedding ceremony "seals the deal" and although the kiss is not a required part of the ceremony, most will agree that this sign of affection is an enjoyable exchange to tie the knot. After the reception there are many opportunities for the bride and groom to kiss and wedding guests are always creative in making them do so. The most traditional way guests entice the new couple to kiss is by clinking their glasses. An ancient Christian tradition explains that the clinking sound scares the devil away and the couple kisses in his absence. Another tradition is to ring bells placed at the tables by the wedding party. A ring of the bell signals the bride and groom to kiss.

FULL-CIRCLE KISSES

(the desired) and (your name here) in a tree
K.I.S.S.I.N.G.
First comes love,
then comes marriage
then comes the baby in the baby carriage

And so it goes, bringing us full-circle kisses back to maternal kisses.

THE GEOGRAPHY OF KISSING

WHERE IN THE WORLD KISSES

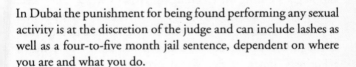

In Dubai, if found guilty of performing any sexual activity in public, one may be whipped, imprisoned and/or deported. In April 2010, two British nationals were sentenced to a month in prison with subsequent deportation and fined about £200 for kissing and drinking alcohol in public.

Arrested on the evidence of a woman who had not seen the kiss herself but had been told about it by her two-year-old child, the pair maintained that they exchanged only a kiss on the cheek as a greeting.

WHIPLASH KISSES

In Dubai the punishment for being found performing any sexual activity is at the discretion of the judge and can include lashes as well as a four-to-five month jail sentence, dependent on where you are and what you do.

CRIMINAL KISSES

In Indonesia new morality laws have criminalized kissing in public. Offenders caught kissing in the open can be jailed for up to ten years, and fined as much as 300 million rupiah ($33,000). Travelers caught kissing in public can face five years in jail. A new anti-pornography bill proposed a ban on "kissing on the mouth in public" and on "public nudity, erotic dances and sex parties."

Obscene Kisses

Still regarded as largely taboo, it is extremely rare to see couples kissing in public in India, although holding hands (among male friends, too) is acceptable. Public kissing brings a twelve-dollar fine in Delhi.

In a place where future spouses often do not meet until the wedding, the notion of courtship is still a novelty for many. "The kiss is the threshold marker," says sociologist Shiv Visvanathan. "It represents the more Western notion of sexual behaviour."[50]

In 2005, an Israeli couple found themselves in court in Rajasthan for kissing after getting married in a traditional Hindu ceremony in Pushkar. Priests were offended when they kissed and hugged during the chanting of religious verses. They were fined a grand total of twenty-two dollars. A year later political opponents called on the chief minister of the state of Rajasthan to resign because she offered a ceremonial kiss of welcome to a businesswoman at the World Economic Forum. In 2007, Hollywood actor Richard Gere sparked riotous protests and the burning of effigies in India after kissing Bollywood actor Shilpa Shetty at an AIDS awareness rally in Delhi. The protesters said Gere had insulted Indian culture by kissing the hand and face of the actress.

---

50   Mark Sappenfield, "In India, a Public Kiss is Not Just a Kiss."

JAILBIRD FOR KISSING

In September 2008, a married Indian couple was arrested by Delhi police and charged with obscenity in a public place. The police officers said the couple was "sitting in an off-putting position near a railway station and kissing, which caused passersby to feel bad." However, in court, the judge decided the young couple's kiss did not break the law and that they did nothing wrong. Judge Muralidhar said, "an expression of love by a young married couple" was not illegal. In addition, he said he wondered how anyone could find a simple kiss to be obscene.[51]

UNDERGROUND KISSES

In Moscow a kissing ban was considered on the Moscow metro. In an attempt to raise levels of public morality, couples caught kissing could be fined under new regulations being considered by city authorities while those going too far could face jail. City education official Tatyana Maksimova complained that "our children are getting love lessons all day long from what they see around them."

---

51 www.theindian.com/newsportal/health/kissing

Great British Reserve

Even in one of the world's most tolerant societies—Great Britain—public kissing has been reigned in. Following concerns that embracing couples were causing congestion, No-Kissing signs appeared at Warrington Bank Quay train station early in 2009. The signs installed as part of a £1m refurbishment of the station have divided the car park and taxi ranks into "kissing" and "no-kissing" zones.[52]

The Greeting Kiss

Salutary kisses and kisses of a non-erotic nature reign supreme over all other gestures of greeting, be they handshakes, hugs, bows, nods and nose rubbing. The application of this platonic kiss is as mercurial as any other (be it dictated by culture, religion or fashion) and reflects one's social class, etiquette and character.

---

52 Mark Hughes, "No Kissing Allowed at Warrington Station—It Blocks the Platform."

Cheek Kissing

In a cheek kiss, both persons lean forward and either lightly touch cheek with cheek, or lip with cheek. Depending on country and situation, the number of kisses is usually one, two, three or four. Hand-shaking or hugging may also take place. Determined by the local culture, cheek kissing may be considered appropriate between a man and a woman, a parent and child, two women or two men. Regarding the latter it may, however, bring up associations with homosexuality.

Air Kisses

A variant of the cheek kiss is the air kiss. This kiss is performed without actually making contact with the skin, but with the lips fairly close to the cheek. A kiss may also be blown from a distance of several feet. This is most often done as flirting, but it can also be done sarcastically ("mwah, mwah…"). Cheek kissing is very common in Southern Europe, the Mediterranean, the Middle East and Latin America.

A Plague on Kisses…

Most recently the practice of this greeting has come under attack, not by rigid moralists but by the outbreak of the H1N1 virus. Across Europe general warnings have been issued but not yet legally enacted.

AU REVOIR TO *LA BISE*

In France the practice of planting a kiss on each cheek to say hello or goodbye, known as *la bise,* was put in jeopardy by the outbreak of Swine Flu in 2009. The French Health Ministry warned everyone to avoid the ritual, fearing the flu pandemic would grow worse as winter approached. The ban was put into effect in two schools in the town of Guilvinec, in France's western Brittany region where as a playful alternative to *la bise,* teachers set up *"bise* boxes" pupils slipped heart-shaped greetings inside before they were exchanged in class.

Following the death of Italy's first victim from Swine Flu, worshippers in Naples were told they could no longer kiss a phial said to hold the blood of a saint because of fears of spreading the virus. Instead, the congregation at the city cathedral was touched on the forehead by the phial on the September 19 feast of St. Januarius.

"If the ban crosses the Channel," wrote the *Daily Mail,* "it could come as a relief to some Britons who have never been comfortable with *la bise* anyway." [53]

CHEEKY CUSTOMS

IN THE LANDS OF THE FREE AND SOMEWHAT EASY
(The Americas)

---

53 Peter Allen, "Why Swine Flu Means French Can Kiss Goodbye to Their Friendly Greeting."

"Kisses are the language of Love—so lets talk it over."
American Proverb

In general, there is a relaxed attitude to kissing across the United States and Canada. Despite a puritanical legacy (see History Section, Blue Laws, p. 116) this has diminished somewhat as immigrant groups (especially those from Latin American and Southern Europe) brought their kissing customs with them. Farther south in Latin America, cheek kisses between men and women are universally customary, even at first encounter. Less acceptable are cheek kisses between two men, bar in the case of father and son. To kiss *a la Italiane* denotes acceptable non-homoerotic kisses between men, for example, kisses like those of winning soccer players.

PAN–EUROPEAN KISSES
—One, Two, Three or Four...

Across much of Europe, cheek kissing is the norm. Kisses planted a specific number of times could theoretically denote one's country of origin. However, kissing traditions can differ between neighboring towns, so the following is a general overview of customs.

In France it is traditional to start on the right cheek and one can continue alternating cheeks up to four times, though standard practice allows for two, one on each cheek. In Italy, there are no rules regarding how many kisses or from which cheek one must commence. Three is the lucky number for the Swiss and Dutch, who like to start and end on the same cheek. The Belgians kiss according to age and regard those with more years upon them as deserving more kisses. The Scandinavians, Austrians and Spanish are of the two-time type of kissers. The Germans, slightly more formal, reserve their kisses for family and close friends. In Britain only recently has the greeting kiss once more overtaken the friendly slap on the shoulder or shake of the hand. Kissing was considered a serious matter in Russia, a kiss bestowed by the Tsar being the ultimate sign of recognition. In Turkey, it is completely normal for men to kiss each other.

Middle Eastern Kisses

In the Middle East there is a long tradition of elaborate greeting kisses albeit in public and only between men. These kisses carry no homosexual connotations. Of the more liberal Arab countries, for example, Lebanon and Egypt, cheek kissing between men and women is accepted in some circles.

Kissing is extremely uncommon in Southeast Asia, especially in countries with predominantly Buddhist or Hindu cultures. In Indonesia, Malaysia, India and Pakistan kissing in public is not acceptable and the Nepalese don't kiss at all.

In Macau, an Old Portuguese colony, cheek kisses are a remnant of former colonial customs and remain in practice. The Filipino and Thai are also partial to a kiss or two. Although in the Philippines, it is a cheek-to-cheek kiss, not lips-to-cheek.

Traditionally the Japanese preferred to bow and the Chinese and South Koreans were disinclined to kiss at all but over time, these countries have been exposed to Western ways and have begun to adopt this kissing habit.

THE PHYSICAL GEOGRAPHY
OF A KISS

WHERE X MARKS THE SPOT

Forehead Kissing
Conveys a blessing
or reverence

Cheek Kissing
Salutory

Lip Kissing
Salutory

Ceremonial
Ring Kissing

Devil's Kisses

Hand
Kissing

Hemline Kisses

Thigh Kissing
Vassels sometimes
kissed a Lord's
thigh

Pope's Toe

Subjugation
Subservience

The ground beneath your feet

III

THE HISTORY OF KISSING

THIS SECTION does not claim in any way to provide the reader with a comprehensive representation of the kiss in history, the history of the kiss or indeed an A–Z of historical kisses. Much as I would have liked to, I confess I have barely scratched the historical surface of the gesture; bound by subjectivity, context and wrapped in a complex maze of nuances and subtleties. I must also admit to a total bias toward the history of the Christian Western world and to focusing on England in particular.

Instead, the following will be (in an approximation of chronological order) subjective snapshots of the kiss in different guises throughout the past, independent from its wider cultural significance. The sort of kisses concerning us here are the mystical, venerable, peaceful, religious, ceremonial kisses: kisses of homage, subjugation, deference, obedience, respect, loyalty, healing and conciliatory kisses, political, scandalous and transgressive kisses, those of betrayal, murder and death.

TIME IMMEMORIAL KISSES

The first recorded kiss was traced to 1500 B.C. India by anthropologist Vaughn Bryant. Early Vedic scriptures mention people "sniffing" with their mouths, and later describe lovers "setting mouth to mouth." It is thought that the kiss made its way westward when Alexander the Great conquered the Punjab over a thousand years later.

Pagan Kisses

Since the dawn of consciousness, sun and moon have been greeted with kisses of veneration, paid by lip service to various gods, idols, icons and artifacts.

Renaissance monk Fra Colonna, enamored of pagan ways, argued passionately about the origins of many modern ecclesiastical customs.[54]

"Kissing of images, and the Pope's toe is Eastern Paganism. The Egyptians had it of the Assyrians, the Greeks of the Egyptians, the Romans of the Greeks, and we of the Romans, whose Pontifex Maximus had his toe kissed under the Empire. The Druids kissed the High Priest's toe a thousand years B.C. The Mussulmans, who, like you, profess to abhor Heathenism, kiss the stone of the Caaba: a Pagan practice. The Priests of Baal kissed their idols so," and continuing wrote, "…The heathen vulgar laid their lips there first, for many a year, and ours have but followed them, as monkeys their masters. And that is why, down with the poor heathen!"[55]

Classical Kisses

In the early Greek world wives or girlfriends were not always kissed in the romantic way they are now. Classical texts do refer to the "kiss embrace" in relation to prostitutes, whose kisses were akin to oral sex, and in relation to friendships among the male elite where kisses were a sign of regard, albeit eroticized. The

54 *The Galaxy.* Volume 0016, Issue 2 (August 1873).
55 Charles Reade, *Cloister and the Hearth.*

farewell kiss bestowed by Pericles on his wife in Aspasia in fifth century B.C. Athens, was thus regarded as a little "unmanly."[56]

In Hellenistic and Roman times heterosexual kissing obtained an erotic significance via love poetry, although men were always the kissers and women the kissees. Moreover, kissing was used as a symbol of power. Herodotus (i134), in speaking of their manners and customs, says, "if Persians meet at any time by accident, the rank of each party is easily discovered: if they are of equal dignity they salute each other on the mouth; if one is an inferior, they only kiss the cheek; if there be a great difference in situation, the inferior fall prostrate on the ground."

There was a definite hierarchy established in the practice of kissing; the lower one's rank, the nearer the ground; only equals would ever kiss face-to-face. Similarly, under the Roman emperors, kissing conferred a particular status on a subject.

WORSHIPPING KISSES

Greeks and Romans also used the kiss in worship. They believed that breath was the life of man and that giving part of the breath to the adored object represented a sacrifice. Cicero informs us in one of his speeches that the lips and beard of the famous statue of Hercules at Agrigentum were worn away by the kisses of devotees:

> "It is so beautiful that its open mouth and chin are a little worn down because when praying and offering thanks they tend not only to worship it but actually kiss it."[57]

---

56 Harriet Swain, "A Kiss and Tell Story."
57 Marcus Tullius Cicero, *In Verrem (Against Verres)*.

The historian Bayle tells us that a physician, when asked why a woman's lips do not similarly wear away, replied that statues were kissed for centuries and a woman only as long as her beauty lasted.

Punishment Kisses

At the time of the Younger Pliny, Christians who had been arrested were forced to perform *adoratio* (the Roman form of homage and worship), which consisted of raising the right hand to the lips, kissing it and then waving it in the direction of the adored object. That the kiss then became an integral part of the Eucharist for early Christians is surely something of an irony.

Biblical Kisses

It is primarily from scholarly and sacred texts that the kiss may be traced throughout history; within the Bible eight types of kisses are mentioned.

SALUTATION

Greet all the brethren with a holy kiss. 1 Thess. 5:20.
Salute one another with a holy kiss. Romans 16:16.

VALEDICTION

The Lord grant you that ye may find rest, each of you in the house of her husband [Naomi to her daughter-in-law.] Then she kissed them; and they lifted up their voice, and wept. Ruth 1:9.

RECONCILIATION

So Joab came to the king, and told him: and when he had called for Absalom, he came to the king, and bowed himself on his face to the ground before the king: and the king kissed Absalom. 2 Samuel 14:33.

SUBJECTION

Kiss the Son, lest he be angry, and ye perish from the way, when his wrath is kindled but a little. Psalm 2:12.

ADORATION

And stood at his feet behind him weeping, and began to wash his feet with tears, and did wipe them with the hairs of her head, and kissed his feet, and anointed them with ointment. Luke 7:38.

APPROBATION

Every man shall kiss his lips that giveth a right answer. Prov. 24:26.

TREACHERY

Now he that betrayed him gave them a sign, saying Whomsoever I shall kiss, that same is he; hold him fast, and forthwith he came to Jesus, and said, Hail, Master; and kissed him. Matt, 26:48–49.

AFFECTION

When Laban heard the tidings of Jacob, his sister's son, he ran to meet him, and embraced him, and kissed him, and brought him to his house. Gen. 29:13.
Moreover he [Joseph] kissed all his brethren, and wept upon them. Gen. 45:15.

And Joseph fell upon his father's face, and wept upon him, and kissed him. Gen. 1:1.

RELIGIOUS KISSES
—for the love of God

Since ancient times, respect for documents containing the word of God has been shown by raising them to the forehead and kissing them, in submission to his commands. In 1999 Pope Jean Paul II caused quite a stir when he kissed the cover of the Koran.

Common to all major religions is the touching, holding or kissing of sacred books. Hindus swear on the Sanskrit HarivaMa; Muslims on the Koran; Jews on the Torah; Christians on the Bible; Sikhs on the Granth.[58]

KOSHER KISSES

It is written in the Old Testament that Rabbis did not permit more than three kinds of kisses: the kiss of reverence, of salutation and dismissal. In the practice of the faith, it is traditional for Jews to kiss the *sisith* of the *tallith* (prayer shawl) and the *mezuzah* (encased prayer) at the door when entering and leaving home, and the *torah* (holy scroll). It is customary to kiss a sacred book that has been dropped. Jews will also kiss the Western Wall of the Holy Temple in Jerusalem.

---

58 Alfred Ernest Crawley, *Studies of Savages and Sex*.

HAJJ KISSES

Notable kisses in Islam come after praying (*dua*) when it is customary for some Muslims—having brushed their palms over their face—to then kiss the back of their hands, and also when on pilgrimage to Mecca. It is then that the sacred black stone and the four corners of the Kaaba are kissed. The black stone is believed by Muslims to be one of the stones of paradise and to have been blackened by the kisses of sinful but believing lips.

CHRISTIAN KISSES

"SALUTE ONE ANOTHER WITH A HOLY KISS."

Of the great monolithic religions, the kiss has been most prominent in Christianity. The baptized are kissed, as are the newly ordained, the bishop during consecration and the king when crowned; penitents are kissed after absolution and the kiss of peace is given to one and all.

In the early church, kissing was a common form of greeting, irrespective of age, sex or social status. In the works of St. Augustine we find an account of four kinds of kissing: the first, *the kiss of reconciliation* was exchanged by enemies wishing to become friends; the second, *the kiss of peace* was exchanged in church when the Eucharist was celebrated; the third kind *the kiss of love*, loving souls gave to one another, and finally *the kiss of salutation* was given to those to whom they showed hospitality.[59]

---

59 George J. Manson, *Kissing and the Art of Osculation*.

RELIC KISSES

The kissing of relics was also widespread. Relics could take the form of saints' bones, icons, the Gospels, the cross, blessed palms, candles, the hands of the clergy and nearly all the utensils and vestments connected with the liturgy. The celebrant also kissed the altar repeatedly during Mass.

HOLY CROSS KISSING

Kissing the Cross is said to bring blessings and happiness. It was customary in Southern France for people in troubled times to kiss their thumbs, laid in the form of a cross, if no crucifix was available.

BACCIAMANO & PESCTORIO KISSES

Bacciamano (literally *kiss hand*) relates to the ancient custom of kissing the hand or ring of a bishop. *Pesctorio* (or fishing) kisses relate to the Pope's ring, known as the ring of fishermen, so-called because St. Peter (of whom the Pope is believed to be the spiritual heir) was known as one of the "fishers of men." Mark 1:17.

Today, Catholics pay respect to the reigning Pope by kneeling before him and kissing his ring and it is still customary in Southern Italy for people to kiss the hands of their priest.

The Kiss of Power

⌒

"Upon my mouth shall all my people kiss."[60]

So said Pharoah when investing Joseph with supreme authority as his Grand Vizier (prime minister). The Pharaoh then gave Joseph his ring, which represented the Great Seal of Egypt by which royal assent was given to all state documents. Thus was set the precedent of kissing the monarch's ring and investing it with executive power. (Incidentally, the word "mouth" occurs in this Scripture as a synonym for commandment.[61])

Feet Kisses and Such Like...

⌒

"Kings shall lick up the dust of thy feet."[62]

The veneration shown in the kissing of a person's hand or hem is emphasized in the kissing of the feet. A sign of humbleness and an act of servitude, this Christian ritual originated with Mary Magdelene kissing Christ's feet, having washed them with her tears.

The public exchange of such a kiss was of great ceremonial importance. Practiced from Roman times, it was adopted at an early date by the papal court. Examples of the significance of this gesture may be found in the quarrels of Henry II with Thomas à Beckett and of Richard the Lion Heart with St. Hugh of Lincoln.

---

60 Genesis 41:40. Neil M. A. James, *Kissing, Its Curious Bible Mentions*.
61 Genesis 45:21. Ibid.
62 Isaiah 49:23. Ibid.

In the latter case the bishop is recorded as having taken hold of Richard by his mantle and shaking him for failing to offer the formal kiss. The king, overcome by such a display, recovered his good humor and bestowed on the saint the necessary salute.

Beyond the realms of religion, kissing the feet was practiced during European coronation ceremonies and was accepted as an act of fealty and honor. When Rolf the Ganger was receiving the Dukedom of Normandy from Charles the Simple in 911 A.D., he was obliged to kneel and kiss the king's foot. Rolf took the oath but in true Viking style disregarded the rest of the ceremony and appointed one of his followers to pay homage. "The Northman as proud as his master, wilfully misunderstood and instead kissed the monarch's feet by lifting them to his mouth, so as to upset king and throne together, amid the rude laughter of his countrymen."[63]

The kissing of feet ceremony was also used as a sign of humility to the highest of all sovereigns—God. It was customary for English monarchs to kiss the feet of the less fortunate in imitation of Christ, who washed the feet of his disciples and then commanded them to "wash one another's feet." On Maundy Thursday at the start of Lent, the king would tend to the feet of as many poor people as he numbered in years.[64] Clothes, food and money were then distributed among the poor. James II was the last English monarch to perform this in person and it was afterward performed by an almoner. (The practice lives on in the form of Maundy money, which is still given to the deserving poor at the behest of the queen.)

---

63 C. C. Bombaugh A.M. M.D., *The Literature of Kissing.*
64 Ibid. p. 58.

DUSTY KISSES—ALL CONQUERING

Pope John Paul II was known for his ritual of prostration and kissing of the earth (or tarmac) on his arrival abroad. It showed respect and humility, but it could also be interpreted as a symbolic taking possession of the community, as historically expressed in the "aggregation (or appropriation) rite" of kissing the soil. Take, for example, the early eleventh-century crusade of Godfrey de Bouillon. When they came within sight of Jerusalem, the Crusaders are said to have fallen to their knees, weeping and giving thanks and even kissing the sacred earth. In the 1490s, Columbus and his fellow conquistadors, too, reverently kissed the ground when they stepped on the beach of San Salvador.[65]

PAPAL TOE KISSING

In his treatise *De altaris mysterio*, Innocent III (Pope from 1198 to 1216) explains the significance of this curious ceremony: it demonstrates "the very great reverence due to the Supreme Pontiff as the Vicar of Him whose feet were kissed by a woman who was a sinner," and as such became the normal salutation for those granted a private papal audience. However, this gesture, also known as "kissing the slipper," was regarded as humiliating by many of high rank (undoubtedly the sentiment of Rolf the Ganger, noted earlier), and over time the phrase has come to mean obsequiousness.

In an old German war song against Charles V (1506–1556) we find:

---

65 Ibid. p. 52.

Ah think the whole imperial race
Through Popery fell in sore disgrace
And German might was riven
Will you for all their knavery
To slipper kiss be given?[66]

What must almost certainly be an apocryphal story gives an entirely different origin for the custom of kissing the Pope's toe. Apparently it arose from an extreme demonstration of abstinence. In his *History of Civilization in England,* Henry Thomas Buckle tells us that it had been usual to kiss the hand of his Holiness, but toward the end of the eighth century a certain lewd woman, in making an offering to the Pope, not only kissed his hand, but also pressed it. The Pope (possibly Leo III), seeing the danger, cut off his hand, and thus escaped contamination. Since that time, the precaution had been taken of kissing the Pope's *toe,* instead of his hand. And lest anyone doubt the accuracy of this account the historian assures us that the hand, which had been amputated five or six hundred years before, still existed in Rome and was preserved in its original state.[67]

THE JUDAS KISS

"Faithful are the wounds of friends," so says the Old Testament, "but the kisses of an enemy are deceitful."[68]

The Judas kiss, although not the first or only kiss of death mentioned in the Bible, ranks as one the most infamous of

---

66 Christopher Nyrop, *The Kiss and Its History.*
67 C. C. Bombaugh AM. MD., *The Literature of Kissing.*
68 Proverbs 27:6.

kisses ever.[69] For over 2000 years the name *Judas* has been synonymous with betrayal, treachery and shame. Such is its potency, that even to this day it is rare to find someone named Judas. By inverting the symbolism of the kiss (perceived as a gesture of goodwill, a positive, holy and intimate act) Judas's betrayal of Christ appears all the more dramatic and despicable. After all, when identifying Christ, Judas could just as easily have pointed to him.

Although the four Gospels are riddled with discrepancies and contradictions regarding events, the basic premise is that Jesus predicted his own betrayal at the Last Supper, after which he and his disciples went to the Garden of Gethsemane. It was here that Judas Iscariot, working as an informer with a group of soldiers, identified Christ with a kiss. Despite Christ announcing his impending betrayal he did nothing to stop it, and thus it could be argued that it was Jesus who set Judas up.[70]

As for Judas's fate, it is written that he bought a field with the ill-gotten blood money but even so, there could be no peace for him. The medieval epic *Golden Legends* tells how Judas "burst asunder in the midst, and all his bowels gushed out, but he did not vomit them from the mouth because his mouth could not be defiled having touched the glorious face of Christ."

---

69 In the Old Testament General Joab cloaked his murderous intents with a kiss of salutation and thus killed his rival Amasa.

70 Adrienne Blue, *On Kissing*.

PAX KISSES

"WHAT PRAYER IS COMPLETE IF DIVORCED FROM THE HOLY KISS?"[71]

Since the days of the early Church, Christians exchanged a holy kiss of peace as a symbol of their unity in Christ. By the fifth century it had assumed its place after the Lord's Prayer and just before communion.

However from a very early stage the potential abuses of this form of salutation were keenly (not to mention hotly) suspected. Circa 175 A.D., early Christian philosopher Athenagoras of Athens warned that:

> "If anyone kisses a second time it has given him pleasure [he sins]… Therefore the kiss, or rather the salutation, should be given with the greatest care, since if there are mixed with it the least defilement of thought, it excludes us from eternal life."

Clement of Alexandria, c. 195 A.D. also decried its misuse:

> "But there are those who do nothing but make the churches resound with a kiss, not having love itself within. This very thing, the shameless use of a kiss, causes foul suspicions and evil rumors. The apostle calls the kiss holy."[72]

---

71 Tertullian (c. 145–220).
72 www.apostolicchristianchurch.org/Pages/Beliefs,%20The%20Holy%20Kiss.htm.

Kiss Money

∽

…was the term applied to another sort of pax whereby members of a church congregation kissed a picture of a saint for a small fee called "kiss money" or "book money."

Kissing Boards

∽

The latent ambiguity of the holy kiss eventually led to its downfall. Despite church congregations being segregated according to gender, the kiss was still unable to shake off its carnal associations.

> I told the maid that she was fair;
> I've kissed the Pax just after her.[73]

From the end of the twelfth century the use of the *instrumentum pacis* or *osculatorium* (known in English as the "pax board" or "pax brede") was gradually introduced enabling the laity to kiss the board instead of each other. The board was a little plaque of wood (sometimes precious metal or ivory) decorated with pious carving. An English innovation of the thirteenth century, it had spread to the continent and replaced the traditional face-to-face kisses a century later.

---

73 Christopher Nyrop, *The Kiss and Its History*.

Leperous Kisses

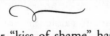

Kisses of utter humility were those bestowed on lepers, as exemplified by St. Francis of Assisi, who meekly kissed a leper's hands. The affliction then vanished, revealing the man as Christ. Leper kissing became fashionable among medieval ascetics and the religious nobility. The Hapsburgs were reputed to heal stammering children by a mouth kiss. Eleanor of Aquitaine (1122–1204) indulged in the practice, and the crusading knights in Jerusalem are said to have paused from the slaughter of infidels to kiss the lesions of the Holy Land's lepers, whose suffering was envied because suffering would bring one closer to God.[74] Kissing lepers was a form of masochism, carrying with it the possibility of inflicting upon oneself the deadly infection, a kiss of death as it were. Leper kissing reached its apogee in the twelfth and thirteenth centuries, to be replaced by witch hunting.

Heretical Kisses

The *osculum infame* or "kiss of shame" has always been associated with heretics. In his text *Octavious Felix* late second-century Christian apologist Minucius Felix has a pagan character set out the rumored practices of his Christian neighbors. Reportedly they worshipped the head of a donkey and reverenced the genitals of their priests. Similar accusations had traditionally been made against the Jews and conspirators against the Roman Empire.

---

74 Adrienne Blue, *On Kissing*.

The kiss of shame (alongside ritual infanticide, cannibalism, orgies and sexual abandon) reemerged in the twelfth century in propaganda against the Cathars and Waldensians, both Christian sects who still practiced the holy kiss. By this time the Devil featured prominently in descriptions and illustrations of the alleged kiss of shame, usually in the form of an animal, *(goat or cat)* who received adoration, worship and a kiss on or around its posterior.

BEWITCHING KISSES

The most infamous witch-hunt manual, the *Malleus Maleficarum,* was written in 1486 by James Sprenger and Henry Kramer. Used as a judicial case book for the detection and persecution of witches, it mentions a woman (whom the author had not, incidentally, been able to bring to trial) who apparently added the words, "Give me the tongue in the arse" to the blessing bestowed on the people during mass.[75]

In Eichstatt, a Prince-Bishopric in southeastern Germany, prosecutors attempted to cajole the female defendants in witch trials to admit to the shameful act of kissing the Devil's rectum during the Sabbath. In 1590 news from Scotland describing the Scottish witches' attack on James VI reported the confession by the witch Agnes Sampson that the Devil "enjoined them all to a penance which was that they should kiss his buttocks in sign of duty to him; which being put over the pulpit bar, every one did as he had enjoined them."[76]

---

75 Jonathan Durrant, "The Osculum Infame: Heresy, Secular Culture and the Image of the Witches' Sabbath."
76 Ibid. p. 40.

Naturally these salacious "confessions" appealed to a wide audience, something enabled by the advent of the printing press in the 1440s. In 1570 a prominent illustration in a news sheet reporting the witch trials in Geneva showed a woman bending to kiss the backside of a devil.

Tail-End Kissing

Medieval literature makes much of kisses which tread the fine line between the social and the sexual, using them as the basis for drama, both tragic and comic. For example, in Chaucer's *The Miller's Tale* the kiss is employed by way of comic humiliation. Alison, the adulterous wife, is pestered at night by her lover Absalon who desires a kiss. Alison obliges by sticking her hole (Chaucer's terminology) out of the window whereby "Absalon put up his mouth and kissed her arse, most savorously before he knew of this."[77]

Detestable Kisses

In the *Coelifodina* of 1502 the holy kiss is laid bare. Kisses of the body are defined thus: as praiseworthy, excusable or detestable. The *osculum detestabile* was categorized as a kiss of dissimulation, betrayal and lust (Freud would surely comment on the fact that lustful kisses received the longest commentary). It was now clear that the sins summarized under the *osculum detestabile* had begun to surround the holy pax kiss as well, since how could the

---

77 Geoffrey Chaucer, "The Miller's Tale."

kiss be at once sacred, profane, spiritual, erotic, a sign of peace and a source of discord?

Questionable Kisses

By 1512 the demise of the pax kiss had been set in motion: omitted from traditional mass on Maundy Thursday and in some cases on Good Friday and Easter Saturday, the kiss of peace even proved too loaded a gesture to be practiced during the commemoration of Christ's Passion on Easter Sunday, as, inherently, it would call to mind the Judas kiss.

Reforming Kisses

Fundamental to the pax had been the belief that public gestures could and should connect body and spirit. However during the Reformation, Luther and his followers reinterpreted this link. Luther argued that "…honouring God with kisses and other gestures…if it is not done in the heart through faith it is nothing but an illusion and trickery."[78] From 1520 onward Protestants omitted the kiss altogether. This coincided with the disappearance of other forms of ceremonial kissing.

---

78 Craig Koslofsky, "The Kiss of Peace in the German Reformation."

Disappearing Kisses

In the Middle Ages everyone, be they a vassal or a lord, had paid homage to their betters with a kiss.

Naturally, vassals (or servants) had done so in a more demeaning way by kissing their lords on the thigh as well as the hands, and in the lord's absence, kissing the door (*baiser l'huis* or the bolt *baiser le verrouil*) although this eventually became seen as an abasement too far.[79]

Likewise, during the fifteenth and sixteenth centuries, the kiss died out as a symbol of reconciliation, to be replaced by sworn oaths and documents. Evidently the uncomfortable associations of the same-sex kiss had begun to undermine it.

Platonic Kisses

Nowhere was this shift more evident than in Renaissance scholarship. Scholars rendered Plato's philosophy of love entirely consistent with contemporary Christian morality by reasoning that his love for boys was of a non-sexual kind—hence the emergence of Platonic love as an ideal. As if to make the divide between the sexual and non-sexual plainer still, the kiss became more identifiably erotic—and also perhaps more attractive as advances in dentistry were made.[80]

---

79 Christopher Nyrop, *The Kiss and Its History*.
80 Helen Berry, "Lawful Kisses? Sexual Ambiguity and Platonic Friendship in England c.1660–1720."

IN THE EYE
OF THE BEHOLDER KISSES

Princess Margaret of Scotland astonished her courtiers by kissing the ugly poet Alain Chartier (c. 1392–1430), "for nature had, so far as Chartier was concerned, suffered a beautiful and rich mind to take up its abode in an ugly body." The princess replied it was not the man she had kissed but the mouth from which so many golden words had proceeded. Therefore her kiss was an expression of respect and one we would now term *platonic*.[81]

COR BLIMEY GUV'

The rapid shift in courtly manners and acceptable practice can be seen by comparing two accounts of behavior that were written perhaps half a century apart, first that of Desiderius Erasmus (c. 1466–1536) and then that of Michel de Montaigne (1533–1592) (see p. 112). According to Renaissance humanist scholar Erasmus, the fifteenth-century English attitude to kissing was evidently far more relaxed than that of the twenty-first century in that salutary kisses were planted on the lips. So much for English reserve! Writing in summer of 1499 to his poet friend Fausto Andrelini in Italy, Erasmus said:

"If you did but sufficiently know, my Faustus, the pleasures of England, you would haste hither with wings at your feet, or if your gout would not permit you to do that, you would wish yourself a Dedalus. To mention only one pleasure out of multitudes: here are nymphs

---

81 Christopher Nyrop, *The Kiss and Its History.*

beautiful as angels, lovely and debonair; you would readily confess that your muses are not to be compared to them. Besides, we have a custom which can never be sufficiently commended. Wherever you go, you shall be welcomed with kisses from them all; and when you depart, you shall be dismissed with as endearing a farewell: return the same sweet welcome shall be repeated… In a word, all places you enter are full of kisses, which my friend had you once but tasted, how soft, how fragrant they are, you would not, I am positive, like Solon desire to live ten years, but till death in England."[82]

Continental Kisses

As is suggested by Erasmus, the kiss of salutation or "to greet on the mouth" was a common gesture throughout Europe in the fifteenth and sixteenth century, especially among the nobility.

A letter written in 1544 from Annibale Caro to the Duke of Palma describes the visit of the French Queen Eleonore to the Emperor Charles V in Brussels.

"When we met," he says, "the ceremony of reception with kissing of the ladies was interesting…not only the higher nobility but even all the rest took each his lady, and the Spaniards and Neapolitans were the most eager. It gave rise to much merriment when the Countess of Vertus, Charlotte de Pisseleu, was observed to lean over her saddle to such an extent in order to kiss the Emperor that she slid off her horse and kissed the earth instead of his Majesty's mouth." [83]

82 Ibid. p. 155.
83 Ibid. p. 154.

POETICAL KISSES

> "Twist yielding lips, in every thrilling kiss, To dart the trembling tongue—what matchless bliss!
> Inhaling sweet each others mingling breath, While Love lies gasping in the arms of Death!"[84]

Dutch poet Johannes Secundus was born at the Hague in 1511 and died at Utrecht in 1536. A sixteenth-century Keats, he died aged twenty-five, and his collection of *Basia* or *Kisses* was published posthumously in 1539. The *Basia* rank alongside the lyrics of Catullus and consist of a collection of nineteen poems written in various meters, which explore the theme of the kiss. He elaborates on his central theme with kisses as nourishment or treatment; kisses that injure or kill; and the exchange of souls brought about by the act of kissing.

THE RISE OF THE RESERVE

However, by the time famous French essayist Montaigne was writing (in the mid- to late-sixteenth century) all this kissing had lost its novelty: "It is a highly reprehensible custom that ladies should be obliged to offer their lips to everyone who has a couple of lackeys at his heels, however undesirable he may be and we men are no gainers thereby for we have to kiss fifty ugly women to three pretty ones."[85]

---

84 C. C. Bombaugh A.M. M.D., *The Literature of Kissing.*
85 Christopher Nyrop, *The Kiss and Its History.*

By the end of the seventeenth century, English playwright William Congreve had cause to write "you think you're in the Country where great lubberly brothers slabber and kiss one another when they meet like a Call of Sergeants—'tis not the fashion here."

The distinction between the kiss of affection and kiss of love was much stronger among continental people than in England. As a result, the English social kiss between men and women (which had been on the lips) disappeared, whereas the French kiss on the cheeks was less palpably erotic and so proved more enduring. Likewise any form of kissing between men quickly died out once laws against homosexuality were (re)instituted during the time of Elizabeth I. In 1626 the writer William Vaughan deplored the "unnatural kiss of man with man, a minion-kiss, such as Jupiter used to Ganymede his cup-bearer."[86]

Under the Stuart kings—perhaps notably James I, who was supposedly sexually omnivorous—French influence on courtly manners created a temporary fashion for foppish young men to kiss each other on the cheek. "Sir, you kiss pleasingly," says one of them in an early-eighteenth-century play, "I love to kiss a man, in Paris we kiss nothing else." But in the eighteenth century, men seen kissing were likely to be accused of sodomy.

Affectionate kissing and touching between women friends and acquaintances lasted much longer, because the notion of lesbian love was slower to take root (and was for centuries in fact unrecognized in law) than was that of male homosexual desire.

---

86 Keith Thomas, "Afterword," in *The Kiss in History*.

An Abuse of the Lips

The authors of religious conduct literature argued that adultery began at the point of intent rather than at the moment of actual consummation. In his 1622 tome *Of Domesticall Duties* William Gouge urged careful government of the lips, so that they "delight no in wanton kisses," as part of a whole regimen of bodily control to combat sin.

Mutations of Language

The courtly flourish of kissing a lady's hand as a mark of respect came from the court life of the Renaissance. However, where the practice of social kissing died out, language preserved its memory. The Spaniards say, "I kiss your hands,"[87] and the Austrians, *"Kuss d'Hand."* (A parallel is the kiss of peace, which had first become a regular kiss of greeting, then a spoken salutation: it is still common throughout the world to say *Shalom aleichem*, or *Salem alechem*, peace be with you, the response being *Alechem hasa—lem* with you be peace.)

Misunderstood Kisses

By the same token, the action and meaning of certain words have been conflated at times. In Gaeilge the word *pòg* is derived from the Latin *pax* and means *kiss* not *peace*. Likewise *paz* is

---

87 Alfred Ernest Crawley, *Studies of Savages and Sex.*

medieval Spanish for *kiss,* something most likely originated as a misunderstanding of the priest's words when he kissed the penitent: *Pacem do tibi* (Peace I give unto thee). The penitent may have understood the kiss as the focal point of the ceremony and thought *pacem* referred to that.

DEAR DIARY KISSES

Samuel Pepys's account of his wife Elizabeth's reaction to her discovery of his fondling the maidservant Deb Willet informs us she was more hurt by the fact that he had enjoyed the smaller intimacies of embracing their servant than anything else. Pepys had recorded in his diary on December 22, 1667, "this time I first did give her a little kiss." This "little kiss" was not little in Elizabeth's eyes. It symbolized her displacement both in her spouse's affections and in the household order by an inferior. Equally symbolically, Elizabeth eventually signaled her willingness to mend their broken relationship (once Willet had been dismissed and pronounced a whore by Pepys) by permitting the "kiss of peace."[88]

HISTORICAL KISSES
—just for the record

The longest single work devoted to the kiss is the *Opus Holy Historicum de Osculis* (Frankfurt 1680) written by the German polymath Martin Von Kemp (1642–83). He assembled excerpts

---

88 David M. Turner, "Adultrous Kisses and the Meanings of Familiarity on Early Modern Britain."

from classical, biblical, ecclesiastical, legal, medical and other learned sources to form an encyclopaedic work of over one thousand pages, and listed more than twenty types of kiss.[89]

LEWD AND UNSEEMLY KISSES

Across the pond from England, the law of the Puritans held sway and were known as "blue laws." *Blue* was a slang term for strict behavioral rules, or of a person with deep religious or ethical convictions. An early blue law outlawed kissing in public.

STOCK KISSES

In 1656, a Boston court had sea captain Captain Kemble placed in the stocks for two hours for "lewd and unseemly behaviour" on the Sabbath. His heinous crime had been to kiss his wife in public on a Sabbath, having just returned from a three-year sea voyage. "Wanton dallyances" or even "unnecessary and unseasonable walking in the streets and fields" were punishable offenses. In New London, Connecticut, John Lewis and Sarah Chapman were charged in court with sitting together on the Lord's Day under an apple tree in Goodman Chapman's Orchard.[90]

89 Keith Thomas, "Afterword," in *The Kiss in History*.
90 John Chester Miller, *The First Frontier Life in Colonial America*.

Whipped Kisses

"If you kiss a woman in public though offered as a courteous salutation, if any information is given to the Select members, both shall be whipt or fined." So wrote Edward Ward, a London wit who visited Boston in 1699, and whose racy descriptions of the place and its people were frequently quoted by early historians and writers about the law. Ward also declared, "What a happiness, thought I, do we enjoy in Old England, that cannot only kiss our own wives, but other men's too, without the danger of such a penalty!"

Newton and His Kissing Problem

Newton's "kissing problem" was mathematical. Cambridge University in 1694 saw a famous kissing debate between Isaac Newton and David Gregory; the term *kissing* in this context referring to the game of billiards, and two balls just in contact with one another.

Newton and Gregory disputed the number of identical spheres that could simultaneously make contact with a central ball. Theoretically then it was at most six, but in more recent times the problem had an extra dimension added—how many white billiard balls can kiss a black billiard ball in three-dimensional space?[91]

---

91 http://plus.maths.org/issue23/features/kissing/index.html.

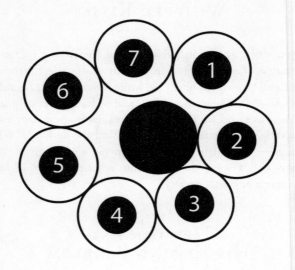

A SERIOUS PROPOSAL
OF THE LADIES
—kissing with intent

BENEDICK: *Peace! I will stop your mouth (doing so with a kiss).*

WILLIAM SHAKESPEARE, C. 1598, *Much Ado About Nothing*

"A Serious Proposal of the Ladies" was a tract written by Mary Astell in 1694, questioning the role of women in society. It challenged the necessity of marriage for all women and revived the Renaissance humanist debates about whether women should be educated or not.

In response, it was encouraged that those who did as Astell suggested be silenced—and not with force but with a kiss. Husbands of unruly wives "stop her mouth with a kiss and show you are no Coward, by not being conquered by a woman's anger, & if you can kiss her whether she will or no, 'twill be a convincing argument that you are still the stronger." January 14, 1696.[92]

Upstairs Downstairs Kisses

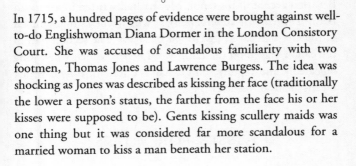

In 1715, a hundred pages of evidence were brought against well-to-do Englishwoman Diana Dormer in the London Consistory Court. She was accused of scandalous familiarity with two footmen, Thomas Jones and Lawrence Burgess. The idea was shocking as Jones was described as kissing her face (traditionally the lower a person's status, the farther from the face his or her kisses were supposed to be). Gents kissing scullery maids was one thing but it was considered far more scandalous for a married woman to kiss a man beneath her station.

Canon Kisses

In 1762 the sweet six-year-old Mozart traveled to Vienna to play for Empress Maria Theresa in the beautiful hall of mirrors at Schönbrunn Palace. After the concert it is said he jumped into the empress's lap where upon he hugged and kissed her. This occasion signaled the beginning of his prodigious fame

---

92 Helen Berry, "Lawful Kisses? Sexual Ambiguity and Platonic Friendship in England c. 1660–1720."

and public kissing of royalty. Later, when taken to Versailles, Mozart tried to kiss Madame de Pompadour, the mistress of Louis XV, but La Pompadour pushed him away. Incensed he wondered, "Who is this that does not want to kiss me?—the Empress kissed me."

Kissing also featured in his canons, illustrating the composer's multilingualism and his taste for lighthearted scatological humor. One such canon in B-flat major with German lyrics is *"Leck Mich im Arsch"* (literally "Lick Me in the Arse" or "Kiss My Arse"). Composed in 1788 as part of a set of ten canons, it contained two bilingual puns. Playing on the strong Bavarian accent of his tenor, Mozart had written in a pseudo-Latin: *Difficile…lectu mihi mars…*, which when sung sounded to the German ear as *leck du mi im Arsch*. The second pun in the canon played on the Latin word *jonicu*, which when sung repeatedly and rapidly sounds like the Italian, *cujoni*, which means "balls or testicles."

KISSES FOR VOTES

In 1784, Georgiana Duchess of Devonshire caused the political scandal of her day when canvasing for the leader of the "Whig" or Liberal party, Charles James Fox.

The notorious incident supposedly took place in late March, and involved the duchess exchanging kisses for votes with men, among whom was a butcher—a commoner. The incident was a gift to the supporters of William Pitt who sought to sully her reputation by constantly referring to her granting favors as a form of prostitution. The incident was predictably fully exploited in the press.

"We hear the D-ss of D grants favours to those who promise their votes and interest to Mr. Fox." The *Morning Post*, dated March 31, 1784.[93]

The duchess's success in the election despite the press campaign was perceived as a danger to the male-only political order and the wider status quo. In an era when politics had become soft and corrupt, there was general consensus that it needed to be reformed and made more "manly" and "pure"; the duchess's respectability had to be undermined so that her political activities could be devalued and dismissed.

KISSING CURRENCY

The duchess was not the first woman or man to use (or be accused of using) this tactic. In a little work published in London in 1758, entitled *A New Geographical and Historical Grammar*, we find the following paragraph covering bribery and kissing:

> "In boroughs the candidates are so wise as to apply chiefly to the wife. A certain candidate for a Norfolk borough kissed the voters' wives with guineas in his mouth for which he was expelled [from] the House; and for this reason others, I suppose will be more private in their addresses to the ladies."

---

93 Elaine Chalus, "Kisses for Votes: The Kiss and Corruption in Eighteenth-Century English Elections."

THE PRINTERS' KISSES

Print on my lips another kiss,
The picture of thy glowing passion;
Nay this wont do—nor this—nor this—
But now—Ah, that's a proof impression!
But yet, methinks it might be mended
Oh yes I see it in those eyes;
Our lips again together blended
Will make the impression a revise.[94]

LAMOURETTE KISSES

In 1792 on July 7 as revolution raged and the Austrian and Prussian armies were marching on Paris, Bishop (or Abbé) Lamourette made a fervent patriotic speech, whereby, in the most moving of terms, he exhorted all the members of the Legislative Assembly to bury their differences. He finished by saying, "Let us forget all dissension and swear everlasting fraternity," and the deputies at once fell into each other's arms and in a universal kiss of reconciliation everyone forgave each other's "wrongs." Sadly this unity did not last long. The quarrels began again the following day, and two years afterward Lamourette died by the guillotine; the expression *un baiser de Lamourette* still survives in the French Language as a half-ironical term for a short-lived reconciliation.[95]

---

94 C. C. Bombaugh A.M. M.D., *The Literature of Kissing.*
95 Christopher Nyrop, *The Kiss and Its History.*

Och Aye Kisses

When the fourth Duke of Gordon raised the infantry regiment of the Gordon Highlanders in 1794, original recruits were drawn from his estates, not least because the Duchess of Gordon is said to have offered a kiss as an incentive to join up. Duncan Mackenzie, a veteran of Waterloo, delighted in relating how he "took the shilling" (for example, signed up) from between her teeth with his kiss.

Emperors' Kisses
—love from the battlefield

Napoleon wrote to his beloved Josephine in 1796, "…I hope before long to crush you with a million kisses burning as though beneath the equator…" and "A kiss on the heart, another one a little lower, another lower still, far lower…"[96]

Fated Kisses

"Kiss me Hardy." Admiral Lord Nelson, 1805

Never has a dying request been so contentious. The story goes that on October 21, 1805, as the Battle of Trafalgar raged, Vice-Admiral Horatio, Lord Nelson, lay dying belowdecks on HMS *Victory*. Close friend and flag captain, Thomas Hardy came to his side and when asked for a kiss he duly obliged, planting one

---

96 Andrea Demirijian, *Kissing*.

on Lord Nelson's cheek. "Now I am satisfied," said Nelson, "thank God I have done my duty." Hardy stood up and after looking down silently at his friend, again knelt and kissed him on the forehead. "Who is that?" asked Nelson, now barely able to see. "It is Hardy." "God bless you, Hardy."

JUST NOT DONE KISSES

An English hero asking another man for a kiss? How terribly embarrassing. For years it was suggested and believed that Nelson actually said "Kismet Hardy," which is Turkish for *fate*. However the events of Nelson's death were recorded in careful detail by surgeon William Beatty in an account published in 1807 and wholly defended by two eyewitnesses, the Rev. Alexander Scott, *Victory*'s chaplain, who had been sitting next to Nelson; and the purser, Walter Burke, who had supported the bed under Nelson. Both heard and recorded Nelson's words.[97]

ABOMINABLE KISSES

A German travel guide advised in 1819, "the kiss of friendship between men is strictly avoided as inclining towards the sin regarded in England as more abominable than any other."[98]

---

97 Arthur William Devis, *The Death of Nelson.*
98 Joan Smith, "Of Mouths and Men."

KISS AND TELL

"I shall not say why and how I became, at the age of fifteen, the mistress of the Earl of Craven. Whether it was love, or the severity of my father, the depravity of my own heart, or the winning arts of the noble lord, which induced me to leave my paternal roof, and place myself under his protection, does not much signify; or if it does, I am not in the humour to gratify curiosity in this manner."

So began the infamous memoirs of Harriette Wilson, subtitled *Beauty, Marriage-Ceremonies, and Intercourse of the Sexes, in all Nations; Systems of Physiognomy, etc.* They appeared in nine installments during 1825 and quickly became a bestseller. Harriette gave her lovers the opportunity to "buy themselves out" of her memoirs, a rather unsubtle form of blackmail to which her lover, Lord Wellington, supposedly responded: "Publish and be damned."

The British government were worried that any revelations she might make regarding George IV could damage the reputation of the already unpopular king. As it happens, George was not mentioned; one can only assume he paid up.

PILLOW TALK KISSES

The furor regarding Wilson's memoirs was perhaps inspired by the knowledge that a lover's memory could be rather less complimentary than her pillow talk: Ninon, the great French courtesan, once reflected that the Marquis of Sévigné had "a soul of boiled beef, a body of damp paper, with a heart like a pumpkin fricasseed in snow."

THE KISS OF ALL KISSES

"No doubt the entwinement in The Kiss, *is pretty enough but it meant nothing to me."*[99]
Auguste Rodin

Dante's "two souls that flutter so lightly in the wind" inspired Rodin's iconic sculpture *Le Baiser,* regarded by many as the "kiss of kisses." Rodin provided the explicit sculpture with a classical pedigree by using Dante's *Divine Comedy* as a literary inspiration. He sets in stone the treacherous kiss of Francesca da Rimini and her brother-in-law, Paolo, their own illicit love inspired in turn by the forbidden adulterous love of Sir Lancelot and Queen Guinevere. A book of the Arthurian legend is clutched in Paolo's left hand in Rodin's sculpture.

"One day for our delight we read of Lancelot,
 How him love thrall'd. Alone we were, and no
 Suspicion near us. Oft times by that reading
 Our eyes were drawn together and the hue
 Fled from our alter'd cheek. But at one point
 Alone we fell. When of that smile we read,
 The wished smile, so rapturously kissed

99 Adrienne Blue, *On Kissing.*

By one so deep in love, then he, who ne'er
From me shall separate, at once my lips
All tembling kiss'd. The book and writer both
Were love's purveyors. In its leaves that day
We read no more."[100]

MARBLE KISSES

Le Baiser was first shown at the Paris Salon of 1898 and was immediately acclaimed. Originally made in 1882 as a half-size clay sculpture to feature in Rodin's series The Gates of Hell, Rodin changed his mind and chose to present it as a work in its own right. At the time the public favored marble, but rather than doing it himself, he hired *practiciens* to carve the piece. Marble specialist Jean Turcan carved the larger-than-life *The Kiss,* which is now in the Rodin Museum of Paris, originally commissioned by the French government in 1887. Two further orders followed Rodin's Exposition Universalle in 1900. The first came from a Danish brewer Carl Jacobsen and the second from American Edward Perry Warren, a classical scholar, who ordered his *Baiser* to come with a penis (the Paris cast has a depression rather than a bulge). Warren exhibited the sculpture in the English town of Lewes, but sadly it was deemed immoral by the townspeople and languished in Warren's carriage house until 1928 when it was bought by the Tate, where it remains today.

An enduring twentieth-century cultural icon (although still the target of prudish censorship), it most recently appeared on British postage stamps in 1995—albeit from the waist up.[101]

---

100 Christopher Nyrop, *The Kiss and Its History.*
101 Adrienne Blue, *On Kissing.*

KINETOSCOPE KISSES

Times were a-changing and at a far more rapid speed than any other age. The innovations of the nineteenth century had a profound effect across the world, perhaps none more so on a cultural level than the capturing of motion on film. A goal pursued by many, it was in 1889 that Thomas Edison succeeded. Filmed in April 1896 at Edison's Black Maria studio, actor John Rice kissed May Irwin in a film simply called *The Kiss*. Heads pressed together, the actors are seen talking lip to lip before John Rice preens his moustache and then, holding his cohort's face, plants a series of nibblish kisses on her. According to Edison film historian C. Musser, the actors staged their kiss for the camera at the request of the *New York World* newspaper, and the resulting film was the most popular Edison Vitascope film of 1896.[102]

Popular it may have been, but Chicago critic Herbert C. Stone pronounced that "neither participant is physically attractive and the spectacle of their prolonged posturing on each other's lips… is absolutely disgusting."

ON BOOK KISSING

STEPHANO: *Here, kiss the book.*

WILLIAM SHAKESPEARE, C. 1610, *The Tempest*

The long-held custom whereby witnesses kissed the Bible when taking the stand was practiced until relatively recently. It came from the belief that a contract is rendered stronger by

---

102 http://www.youtube.com/watch?v=eOrKBmtC75Q.

administering a corporal oath, an oath ratified by contact with a sacred object.

In the English courts, the Houses of Parliament and certain other places, non-Christians are permitted to affirm without kissing the Book due to the struggles of atheist Charles Bradlaugh (1833–91) to take his seat in the House of Commons. First elected in 1880, he was finally admitted to the House in 1886. Previously in 1858, Baron Lionel de Rothschild was the first acknowledged Jew to be admitted to Parliament (as a Jew), and had been allowed to swear on the Old Testament. He had been elected as Whig M.P. for the City of London in 1847. The Oaths Acts of 1888 legalized the position.

By the beginning of the twentieth century this practice began to wane, viewed as an old-fashioned and outdated gesture— it would soon be replaced by the raising of one's right hand, otherwise known as taking the "Scotch Oath."

Under the headline English to Abandon Kissing the Book (January 17, 1909), the *New York Times* cited grubby Bibles as a major factor in its declining popularity.[103] Justice Warrington in the Chancery Division had the solution: "To meet the case of those who desire to kiss the Book," said he, when announcing the new method of holding up the right hand, "I have given directions to have Books with washable bindings."

FACTORY KISSES

Famous for its unusual shape, foil wrapping, patented plume and deliciousness, Hershey's Kisses (American chocolates) were first introduced to the public in 1907 and now more than 80 million

---

103 "English to Abandon Kissing the Book," *New York Times*.

Kisses are produced daily. It is thought the candy was named from the sound or motion of the chocolate being deposited during the manufacturing process. Due to the rationing of silver foil in World War II, the chocolates weren't produced between 1942 to 1949. In 1962 colored foil was introduced rather than the silver. Today, there are a variety of Kisses available in different colors and sizes and flavors of chocolate.[104]

MURDEROUS KISSES

In July of 1916, Hungarian Detective Chief Dr. Charles Nagy received a call from a landlord in Cinkota, a town on the outskirts of Budapest. He had made a gruesome discovery. Outside his rented house, he found several large metal drums left by his previous tenant, Béla Kiss. When he punctured one of the drums, the unmistakable smell of human decomposition met him. Inside the drum was a sack containing the preserved body of a young woman with a full head of long dark brown hair.

Béla Kiss (translating as Bill Small) was a well-regarded young man about town and considered by many a most eligible bachelor. On searching Kiss's secret room though, a mass of correspondence between Kiss and various women was discovered, all concerning marriage. It was revealed that Kiss had received 174 proposals, and had himself offered marriage to 74 of the correspondents. He had first defrauded them, in many cases leaving them penniless, and then proceeded to eliminate at least twenty-four, perhaps even as many as thirty, women and one man.

The body of a naked young woman, strangled and preserved in alcohol, was found in each of the seven metal drums. A

104 http://www.hersheys.com/kisses/.

search of Kiss's home and the grounds ensued, revealing even more bodies.

On the outbreak of World War I, Béla Kiss had been conscripted into military service, but despite notifying the military that Kiss was to be arrested immediately, Nagy never caught his serial killer. In October 1916, Dr. Nagy received conflicting messages from a Serbian hospital claiming first that a solider named Béla Kiss had died, and then that he was still alive. When Dr. Nagy reached the ward the man in Kiss's bed was dead, and *not* Béla Kiss. Somehow Kiss had been warned and had substituted the body of another soldier in his bed.

There followed many more sightings of Béla Kiss around the world. The one to which many people gave credence was that of New York City homicide detective Henry Oswald, who felt certain he had seen Béla Kiss emerging from the Times Square subway station in 1932. Nicknamed "Camera Eye" by other detectives for his brilliant memory for faces, many accepted Oswald's report. But the huge crowd in Times Square prevented him from following the suspect.

TRENCH KISSES

"Let me at once disabuse the eager-eyed Sodomites among my readers by stating emphatically once and for all that there was nothing sodomitical in these relationships."[105]
Richard Aldington

---

105 Richard Aldington, *Death of a Hero*.

In the trenches of the First World War, the norms of physical contact between men changed profoundly. Mutilation and mortality, loneliness and boredom, the strain of constant bombardments, the sense of alienation from home, led to a new level of intimacy between them. Historian Joanna Bourke's work on men and masculinity during the war has documented how men nursed and fed their friends when ill, held each other as they danced and wrapped blankets around each other.[106] Intense bonds were created of a homosocial rather than homoerotic nature and the dying First World War kiss was something picked up by writers of the period. It appears in novels such as Ernest Hemingway's *A Farewell to Arms* and in poems by Robert Browning.

In a culture that demonized homosexuality, wartime relationships were often honorably exempt. For certain, the male-to-male kiss was not unusual in the trenches, mostly in close proximity to danger and death. Rev. Connor wrote on December 22, 1914:

> "I prayed to God for the dear lad. I said, 'I'll give you your mother's kiss.' 'Let me do it to you,' & the dear lad kissed me."[107]

TELEGRAPH KISSES
—'allo… 'allo…

Long before cybersex, there was the much more low-key, though decidedly more stylish telegraph kiss.[108]

---

106 Joanna Bourke, *Dismembering the Male: Men's Bodies, Britain and the Great War*.
107 Santanu Das, "Kiss Me, Hardy: The Dying Kiss in the First World War Trenches."
108 "Telegraph Kisses Are New Fad." *Popular Science*.

"Telegraph Kisses Are New Fad." (*Popular Science*, May, 1938). "Sending kisses by wire is a new use for facsimile telegraph transmission. Recently a New York girl kissed a telegram blank and the lipstick impression was placed on the facsimile transmitter, as at left, to be reproduced for delivery in Chicago."

Telegraph Kisses Are New Fad

SENDING kisses by wire is a new use for facsimile telegraph transmission. Recently a New York girl kissed a telegram blank and the lipstick impression was placed on the facsimile transmitter, as at left, to be reproduced for delivery in Chicago.

SPY KISSES
—I've got my eye on you...[109]

Oh, the power of a perfect pout, flutter of lashes and glimpse of a well-turned ankle. History is peppered with beautiful, intelligent women using their feminine wiles (in many incidences the only option open to them) to seduce men in power into spilling state secrets. Russia was particularly adept at this. Even the genius Albert Einstein was not clever enough to avoid the classic honey trap.

A glamorous Soviet secret agent named Maria Konnenkova dated Einstein in the 1940s in order to gain information on the top-secret Manhattan Project, the U.S. effort to develop the first nuclear bomb. Another female spy, Zoya Voskresenskaya,

109 Irina Titova, "Soviet Spy Who Outwitted Einstein."

was among those who warned Stalin that Hitler was preparing an attack on the Soviet Union. In May 1941, Voskresenskaya, using the name Madam Yartseva, attended a reception for German Ambassador Werner von Schulenburg. While waltzing with Schulenburg, Yartseva noticed gaps on the wall of an adjacent room, where pictures had been removed. A glimpse of a pile of suitcases in the same room and some remarks in the German diplomats' conversations put her on full alert, and confirmed other intelligence about the Nazis' plans. On June 17, five days before the invasion began, Voskresenskaya delivered a report to Stalin. He did not believe her.[110]

CAMP KISSES

Even in the darkest of times the kiss remains a sign of humanity and of the grace of man.

Time correspondent Sidney Olson was there on May 7, 1945, when the U.S. Seventh Army entered Dachau and liberated the 32,000 souls who had survived. The emaciated, barely sane, lice-bitten, typhus-infected, rank, soiled captives chose the universal mark of gratitude, respect and joy to greet their liberators: they kissed them.

Overcome, Olson described how the strange noise he thought at first was the wind in the pines turned out to be the cheering of thousands of men; an inestimable number of men, from all nationalities, they even came upon two Hindus. Engulfed in the arms of a huge Russian, Olson writes how he "kissed all over the U.S. insignia on my coat." Whilst "one little Pole" so elated "ran beside us until he dropped flat, shouting desperately: 'Hello Boys!'"

110 http://petersburgcity.com/news/city/2004/07/28/russian_spies/.

VICTORIOUS KISSES

Photographers should always write detailed captions for their photos. Here's why: Alfred Eisenstaedt's iconic image of a sailor kissing a nurse in Times Square during the celebration to mark V-J Day on August 14, 1945, has no caption.

So, in the decades since, various people have claimed they were the ones captured. In 1980, *Life* magazine counted eleven men who said they were the sailor in the photo, among them a Rhode Island fisherman, a New Jersey history teacher and a Harvard University refrigeration mechanic. The most likely was Glenn McDuffie, 80, of North Carolina. By 1995, three women had claimed to be the nurse in the photo. Of the three, Edith Shain, a kindergarten teacher in Beverly Hills, California, seemed to best fit the bill, and she was photographed by Eisenstaedt for *Life* in 1980.

Eisenstaedt died in 1995. For now, *Life* maintains that the identity of the couple remains a mystery.

The Times Square kiss lives on and has been reenacted and celebrated on an annual basis for several years. In 1996 *The New Yorker* published an imitation of the picture to celebrate gay pride Sunday, subverting the image by depicting two sailors kissing.

KISSES OF MISIDENTIFICATION

Perhaps the most populist romantic image of all is Robert Doisneau's "The Kiss by the Hôtel de Ville," taken on a Parisian street in 1950. Widely reproduced, it depicts two lovers lost in a kiss, oblivious to everything but their shared moment of bliss.

This image certainly evokes a universal feeling, a moment easy to project one's self into, and this is exactly what Denise and Jean-Louis Lavergne did in 1988 when they thought they recognized themselves as the couple. They had been present on that street in 1950 and had a diary to prove it. Denise had even kept the skirt and jacket worn that day and Jean-Louis recognized the blue scarf as one his sister had given him for Christmas. After contacting Doisneau, they were filmed for a documentary, but when the footage of them was cut, they were very upset that they would not have the chance to celebrate their romance with the public. So they went to court to prove that they were the legendary couple. Under French privacy law, they argued their image had been "stolen" by Doisneau, and demanded financial redress.

The photo may have captured a visual representation of true love but it was in no way *true*. It emerged that the image was staged and that the couple were in fact an actress named Françoise Bornet and her boyfriend. Bornet, who had been paid a small sum by Doisneau, attempted to sue for a percentage of the future proceeds.

The court ruled that the kiss could not have been stolen from the Lavergnes for the simple reason that they were not the couple in the photograph.[111]

007 KISSES

The lipstick pistol was a pistol used by the KGB during the Cold War. It was a single-shot 4.5mm pistol hidden inside a lipstick holder, referred to as "The Kiss of Death." The weapon was first detected at a border crossing into West Berlin.

---

111 Adrienne Blue, *On Kissing*.

Lipstick was one of many options for concealing weapons during clandestine operations—flashlights, pens, tobacco pipes and cigarette packets were also used, and the rather unpleasant single-shot Rectal Pistol, which was encased in rubber and hidden precisely where the name suggests. Not something you want to go off prematurely.[112]

AY CARAMBA KISSES

In 1969 an effort was made to crack down on young lovers who were smooching in public in the town of Inca on the island of Majorca. When the police chief began handing out citations that cost offenders 500 pesetas per kiss, a group of 30 couples protested by staging a kiss-in at the harbor at Cala Figuera. Following a massive roundup by police, the amorous rebels were fined 45,000 pesetas and then later released.

ARABIAN KISSES
—the type to lose one's head over!

In 1975, on March 25, King Faisal of Saudi Arabia bowed his head in expectation of a kiss from his nephew Prince Faisal bin Mussad Abdel Aziz. Instead, the prince shot him. Still alive, the king was rushed to hospital. However, doctors were unable to save him, the bullets having penetrated beneath the chin and through the ear.

---

112 http://www.spymuseum.org/about/faq.php.

Prince Faisal bin Mussad was later found guilty of regicide and in June 1975 he was executed by beheading in the public square in Riyadh. The prince's motives remained unclear.[113]

VANDALIZED KISSES

In a case of artistic destructivism, Ruth van Herpen, while visiting the Oxford Museum of Modern Art in 1977, kissed a white monochrome painting by Jo Baer. Leaving a lipstick kiss behind, she was ordered to pay the cost of restoration. At her trial she had argued that she had kissed the "cold" artwork in order to "cheer it up."

COMMUNIST KISSES

Dmitri Vrubel's iconic mural of Leonid Brezhnew kissing Erich Honecker had pride of place at the East Side Gallery, created in 1990 to celebrate the Berlin Wall's collapse after twenty-eight years. The gallery featured works by 118 artists from 24 countries, who used a remaining stretch of the wall as a canvas. However, weather, pollution and vandalism took their toll and Berlin authorities claimed *The Kiss* was beyond repair. Vrubel could simply paint another one, they said.

"These barbarians! My painting has been destroyed," stormed Mr. Vrubel. "I have no problem with restoration but I cannot simply paint a new picture like making a sandwich! They have sold postcards, teacups, coffee mugs, key ring holders around the world with this image on it and I didn't get a cent."[114]

113 http://news.bbc.co.uk/onthisday/hi/dates/stories/march/25/newsid_4233000/4233595.stm.
114 http://www.spiegel.de/international/germany/0,1518,615900,00.html.

KREMLIN KISSES

On December 6, 1992, Russia experienced its first tabloid sex scandal when Daria Aslamova, a 23-year-old journalist, claimed she kissed two of the Congress's best-known heavyweights—50-year-old speaker, Ruslan Khasbulatov, and the 45-year-old leader of the most powerful opposition coalition—in her *Notes of a Naughty Girl*.

Apparently Khasbulatov invited her to look at his pipe collection and plied her with Polish vodka. "He knew women and how to speak to them. He clearly wanted me. And there is hardly a woman in the world that doesn't love the fire in a man's eyes, even if he is a Quasimodo."[115]

MINOR KISSES OF A DUBIOUS NATURE

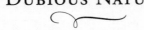

In 1996, Jonathan Prevette, a first grader from Lexington, North Carolina, became famous overnight and appeared on talk-shows across the U.S. His claim to fame? He had kissed a girl on the cheek and had been removed from school on the basis that his act constituted "unwelcome touching." Such was the media storm that the U.S. Department of Education was forced to rewrite their sexual harassment guidelines, omitting kisses by first graders.

---

115 Andrew Higgins, "Kiss and Tell Comes to the Kremlin."

LANA CITRON

Kiss Me, Kill Me

A kiss of death ingeniously bestowed upon an errant lover…

The *Shanghai Daily* reported a vicious revenge taken by a Chinese woman upon her lover, when she killed him with a rat-poison-laced kiss having suspected him of being unfaithful:

> "Xia Xinfeng, from Maolou in the central province of Henan, passed a capsule with rat poison from her mouth to her long-time lover, Mao Ansheng, during a kiss. Mao swallowed the capsule and died soon afterwards.
>
> "The couple had said that if either one of them cheated on the other, he or she would have to die," the paper said in explaining the mouth-to-mouth assault."

Xia found Mao had been "talking" with another woman and deemed that he had broken their promise.

Xia was sentenced to death in September 2007.

IV
CULTURAL KISSES

THE KISS is woven into every fiber of human culture. From nursery rhymes, playground games, traditions, customs, proverbs, it is a staple sweetmeat in the mediums of art, literature, poetry, film, photography, music and sport. Whether symbolically or practically represented, the kiss is prolific, it is everywhere, nowhere, visible, invisible, it is ephemeral, it is patented, it is edible, thirst-quenching, bought, sold, stolen, lauded, decried, it is front-page news, scandalous, sinful, murderous. There is no part of the Western cultural spectrum left unkissed.

ARTFUL KISSES

Whether hewn, drawn, etched or daubed, the kiss has been represented and depicted according to style and taste in every age, from primitive art to the modern day. The following selection spans the kaleidoscope of artistic movements, illustrating various representations of the kiss.[116]

ANCIENT AND CLASSICAL ART

A fifth-century B.C. bowl (from an ancient Greek province, which encompassed Athens) depicts a man and youth kissing. There are many such representations found, especially in vase painting, and thousands of inscriptions celebrating the beauty of youths.

Dating from the fourth- to the second-century B.C. is an Iberian stone relief discovered in Osuna, Spain. It depicts a

---

116 www.oneoffkisses.com.

side view of a couple's meeting of lips and can now be seen in Madrid's National Archaeological Museum.

In India there is a famous eighth-century relief of a kissing couple, found in the rock-cut temple of Kailasa at Elura. The gods Shiva and Shakti (the separated male and female gods) are shown united in an embrace, their pose indicating their need to reintegrate and their act of becoming whole.

MEDIEVAL ART

In early Christian iconography it was common to borrow motifs from well-established pagan myths, reinterpreting and using them as sarcophagi designs. For example, the myth of Psyche (human soul) and Cupid (love)[117] united in divine embrace was very popular. Representing the beautiful Psyche being awakened by a kiss from Cupid, the god of love, it indicated a belief (or hope) in an afterlife in which the Soul enjoys the eternal bliss promised it by Love.

In medieval art the depiction of the kiss was more of a cheek-to-cheek representation than a lip-on-lip display, which was rarely shown. This was so as to portray the face in full or three-quarters view, something that may be observed in many scenes from this period, both in sculptured relief and painting.

FUSION KISSES OR 2-IN-1

The fusion of two bodies appears in a fourteenth-century miniature from a Venetian manuscript, Cecco d'Ascoli's *Acerba,*

---

117 This myth has both Greek and Roman origins. Eros appears in the Greek telling and Cupid is his Roman equivalent.

conserved at the Biblioteca Medicea Laurenziana in Italy. It shows secular lovers kissing and is noteworthy because of the impression it creates of the lovers merging into one. Such depictions are known as "two-in-one" motifs.

In the High Middle Ages, the vice of luxury or lust was commonly represented by a couple embracing and kissing. This type is found in the *luxuria* reliefs of the cathedrals at Chartres and Amiens dating from 1225.

GOTHIC ART

Turning away from the iconic traditions of earlier religious art, Giotto de Bondone (c. 1267–1337) painted what were for his time remarkably realistic scenes, imbuing his subjects with identifiable emotions. In his *Kiss of Judas,* Giotto depicts perhaps the most notorious kiss in human history. In this crammed scene of overlapping figures, Christ and his betrayer face one another. Judas almost completely envelopes Christ in his cloak, as if to render the two men as one. Their gazes and physical closeness are reminiscent of the mesmerizing power of a love kiss and contrast sharply with the violent confusion taking place around them. It is unclear if Judas is about to kiss Christ or has just placed the kiss, but the potency of the kiss is central to the image.

From 1300 to 1310, Giotto completed a number of frescoes portraying the life of the Virgin Mary for the Scrovegni Chapel in Padua. Among these is a representation of Joachim and Anna, Mary's parents, sharing a kiss, a very early example of a man and woman kissing in Western art. Giotto succeeds in depicting a kiss that is both biblical and affectionate.

Renaissance Kisses
—*feeling reborn*

Around 1545, Agnolo Bronzino was commissioned to create a painting that has come to be known as *Venus, Cupid, Folly, and Time*. In it mother and son appear on the verge of a sexual tryst: Cupid fondles his mother's breast and kisses her on the lips. Suggestively, Venus's legs appear to be slightly spread and her tongue is visible. This latter point caused much scandal and at least one owner apparently had it painted out. An astounding painting, it has provoked much scholarly controversy and, to this day, no two art historians agree on the overall idea of the painting.

Neoclassical-style Kisses
—*just like the first time, only better*

Italian sculptor Antonio Canova (1757–1822) is famed for his devotional and mythological pieces. Completed between 1787 and 1793, *Cupid and Psyche* captures the familiar myth (see p. 143), showing the couple on the verge of an embrace. Canova's kiss is perpetually imminent as the pair's lips do not touch.

Rococo

French painter Jean-Honoré Fragonard (1732–1806) had several styles, but was most popular for his whimsically romantic subjects. *The Stolen Kiss* shows an attractive young couple, the woman dressed in a full-skirted lace-and-satin dress, and her would-be lover in the act of kissing her cheek while making a getaway through the window. Through the color of flesh and fabric the picture expresses an indulgence that would have pleased a pre-Revolutionary upper class, and Fragonard's "kissing bandit" is the epitome of Rococo style's impishness.

ROMANTICISM

Franceso Hayez (1791–1882) was a popular Italian portraitist who also rendered historical and allegorical subjects. A particular talent was for capturing the look and feel of opulent cloth, a point that likely drew wealthy sitters who wished to have themselves depicted in their finery. *The Kiss,* painted in 1859, shows a couple, their embrace obscuring their faces in what is obviously a passionate stolen moment. However the eye dwells not on their kiss but on the dazzling quality of the lady's dress, an example of Hayez's virtuosity.

Achille Devéria's *The Harem* illustrated a more transgressive kiss. It shows two women kissing, the kiss applied not to the lips of the face but to ones lower down, and a watcher taking pleasure as well as the participants.

PRE-RAPHAELITES

The Meeting on the Turret Stairs (1864) is one of the better-known works of Irish painter Frederic William Burton. The theme comes from a medieval Danish ballad concerning the tragic affair between Hellelil and her personal guard Hildebrand.

Their love being discovered by Hellelil's father, he orders Hildebrand's death. Hildebrand kills Hellelil's father and six brothers before she intercedes to save the youngest. Hildebrand dies of his wounds and Hellelil herself dies shortly afterward. Burton's work illustrates the final meeting of the lovers. Placing their farewell on the turret stairs, Burton's invention of the kiss on the woman's outstretched arm and the lack of eye contact adds poignancy to the painting.

CHERUB KISSES

L'Amour et Psyché (1890), more popularly known as *The First Kiss,* is a depiction of two kissing cherubs by Adolphe-William Bouguereau (1825–1905). As was common among painters in the second half of the nineteenth century, Bouguereau made a concentrated study of form and technique and drew deeply on classical inspiration. The warmth with which he portrayed children and domestic scenes is a trademark of his style, and this example became a greeting-card classic.

REALISTIC KISSES
—not for the faint of heart

Auguste Rodin's naturalistic style was deemed quite outrageous and crude when first displayed. The couple in *The Kiss* are not idealized, classically nude figures; rather they are naked and openly sexual, although the couple's lips do not actually meet.

IMPRESSIONIST KISSES
—coz you only get one chance to make it count

As one of the originators of the Impressionist movement, Paul Cézanne (1839–1906) is known for his loose energetic brush-strokes. However, an early work, *Kiss of the Muse* (or *The Dream of the Poet*) shows none of the energy with which his paintings are associated and certainly does not suggest Cézanne had been kissed by a muse at this stage.

"AN AMERICAN IN PARIS" KISSES

Mary Stevenson Cassat (1844–1926) was an American artist closely associated with Edgar Degas, among others. Having striven hard, she finally attained some recognition in later life for her work depicting mother-and-child scenes. She succeeded in avoiding the oversentimentality that is often associated with the genre. *Maternal Kiss* depicts a quiet moment of reassurance for a beautiful child in distress.

"GOING IN FOR THE KISS" KISSES
—or "if looks could kill"

Dance at Bougival by Renoir depicts a couple dancing, he seemingly about to kiss her and she looking away, her mouth drooping. Renoir's model was Suzanne Valadon, a famous artist in her own right, who had been a dressmaker before becoming an acrobat and following a fall, an artist's model. A muse and lover of Renoir's, it is thought he depicted her with a drooping mouth as a comment on his own feelings regarding women: their role was either domestic, or providing inspiration for him. His portrayal of her suggests Renoir's uneasiness with Suzanne as an independent-spirited person.[118]

Post-Impressionist Kisses
—the type to leave an aftertaste

Henri de Toulouse-Lautrec (1864–1901) is famous for his works capturing the Paris demimonde of the late nineteenth century. Some of his most intimate paintings are those depicting lesbian embraces among off-duty prostitutes. Mornings and afternoons in brothels afforded women time to relax together and Lautrec's most provocative sketch is *The Kiss* (1892) in which two women are shown on a bed, their bodies closely entwined in a mutual embrace. According to his biographer Julia Frey, Lautrec was especially adept at portraying body language.[119] These figures do not have to speak their love; it is clear from their natural pose.

Abstract Kisses
—obscured intentions

Romanian modernist sculptor Constantin Brancusi (1876–1957) simplified forms in his sculpture, subverting centuries of sculptural tradition, fusing both the influence of his classical training

118   http://blogs.princeton.edu/wri152-3/s06/mgawrys/dance_at_bougival_2.html.
119   Julia Frey, *Henri de Toulouse-Lautrec.*

and his peasant backround. His philosophy of expressing "the idea, the essence of things" drove his artistic conceptions, and his *The Kiss* (1916) bears a resemblance to the statuary of Easter Island in its primitive look.

ART NOUVEAU KISSES

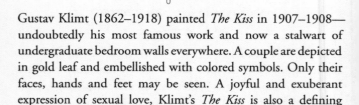

Gustav Klimt (1862–1918) painted *The Kiss* in 1907–1908— undoubtedly his most famous work and now a stalwart of undergraduate bedroom walls everywhere. A couple are depicted in gold leaf and embellished with colored symbols. Only their faces, hands and feet may be seen. A joyful and exuberant expression of sexual love, Klimt's *The Kiss* is also a defining expression of decadence in turn-of-the-century Vienna.

MODERNISM

Marc Chagall began painting *Bouquet aux Amoureux Volants* or *Bouquet of Flying Lovers* (1947) in Paris probably as early as 1933–1934 and worked on it at intervals over many years. The setting is an interior with a big window on the right. The lovers' heads emerge at the top of a bouquet, their bodies concealed behind it. In the top right-hand corner an angel flies through the window with one hand extended toward them. Chagall regarded the picture as one expressing feelings of loss and nostalgia.

Expressionist Kisses

Norwegian painter Edvard Munch (1863–1944), best known for *The Scream*, produced several paintings addressing relationships. His *The Kiss by the Window* (a subject to which he returned again and again) depicts a pair of lovers who are as one to such a degree that their faces dissolve into one another.

Cubist Kisses
—sharp edged

Among the many cubist interpretations of *The Kiss* executed by Pablo Picasso is one painted a day before his eighty-eighth birthday. Whether it is his best is open to debate, but in any case it sold for an eye-watering $15.5 million dollars ($17.4 million after adding buyer's premium) in Sotheby's New York sale room in 2008.

Surreal Kisses
—wow, you blew my mind

In René Magritte's *Lovers* (1928) two lovers kiss, wrapped in shrouds. The symbolism here is of love blinded, the cloth separating the pair as the specter of death envelops passion. As an interesting aside, Magritte's mother drowned when he was a child and when she was found, her nightgown covered her head.[120]

---

120 Adrienne Blue, *On Kissing*.

Pop Art Kisses

The Kiss (1962) by American artist Roy Lichtenstein (1923–1997) amplifies a classic comic-book kiss to iconic proportions. The bold colors and obvious Ben-Day Dots of the printing process recall the advertising and popular press of the day, and in their brazenness challenge the conventions of early 1960s morality.

Warhol Kisses

In 1963 a little-known Andy Warhol bought a silent camera and on 16mm film started recording friends and acquaintances kissing in uninterrupted three- to four-minute takes. This project was to launch his career as an artist. A new kiss was run each week at Gramercy Arts Theater in New York and the resulting series was called Kiss, a fifty-four-minute underground film comprising a montage of the short films spliced together. It featured various couples of various sexes; sometimes the gender of a kisser was undetermined.

LITERATURE

CLASSIC COMIC DRAMA

LYSISTRATA'S KISSES
—withheld for ransom (teasing in the extreme)

In this all-time classic (fifth century B.C.) comedy by Aristophanes, his leading lady Lysistrata urges womankind to refuse their partners' sexual favors so that they may end the disastrous wars between Athens and Sparta. In the following verse she succinctly sums up the lot of womanhood:

…Wars Lewd to the least drop in the tiniest vein,
  Our sex is fitly food for Tragic Poets,
  Our whole life's but a pile of kisses and babies.
  But, hardy Spartan, if you join with me
  All may be righted yet. O help me, help me."

MYTHOLOGY

CUPID AND PSYCHE

Too beautiful for mere mortal men and envied by Venus, Psyche is left on a mountaintop, to wait for her unknown suitor, Cupid, who comes to her veiled in darkness. Thus begins their epic love story. Desperate to discover whom she is kissing, she startles the divine Cupid with the drips of her illuminating oil lamp and he flees. Venus sets Psyche various Herculean tasks, which she manages to complete, and is finally granted divinity, moves to Olympus and marries Cupid. (Perhaps a Lara Croft of former times?)

PARIS AND HELEN

In Homer's *Iliad* Paris and the Spartan queen Helen elope and bring about the fall of Troy when her husband Menelaus seeks revenge for her betrayal. Christopher Marlowe's description of her allure in *Doctor Faustus* has become justly famous:

"Is this the face that launched a thousand ships? And burnt the topless towers of Ilium? Sweet Helen, make me immortal with a kiss. Her lips suck forth my soul: see, where it flies! Come, Helen, come, give me my soul again. Here I will dwell, for heaven be in these lips."

LEGENDARY LOVERS
—the very stuff of folklore

ABELARD AND HELOISE

"Her studies allowed us to withdraw in private as love craved. With our books open before us, more talk of love than books passed between us and more kissing than learning."

The *Story of My Calamities* (c. 1130) by Abelard (1079–1142) tells the tragic story of his affair with Heliose (1100–1163). Between 1108 and 1118, Abelard was a prestigious teacher in Paris. Pupils flocked from all over Europe to hear him; he had, as he tells us, the whole world at his feet. However, his fall from grace was meteoric when he began an affair with Heloise, one of his students and the niece of Canon Filbert. With meticulous detail, Abelard recounts the story: the flight of Heloise to Pallet, where their son was born, the secret wedding, the retirement of Heloise to the nunnery at Argenteuil and the brutal vengeance of the canon, Abelard's castration.

LANCELOT AND GUINEVERE

The kiss conferred by the adulterous queen upon a knight, embedded in legend and folklore, came to have an eternal echo in Dante's *Divine Comedy:*[121]

"And the Queen extends her arms to kiss and embracing him presses him tightly against her bosom, drawing him into the bed beside her and showing him every possible satisfaction as they kiss and fondle each other that in truth such a marvellous joy comes over them as was never seen or known."[122]

TRISTAN AND ISEULT

This romantic tragedy tells of the doomed love story between Cornish knight Tristan and the Irish princess Iseult. Their first passionate kiss occurs after they have inadvertently drunk a love potion. It is an ecstatic lovers' kiss and seals their fate even unto death.

"One body, one life are we… Now come here and kiss me. Tristan and Iseult, you and I, we two are forever one and undivided substance. May this kiss be a seal (confirming) that I remain yours and you mine, constant until death but Tristan and one Iseult."[123]

---

121 Nicolas J. Perella, *The Kiss Sacred and Profane.*
122 Chretien de Troyes, *Lancelot the Knight of the Cart.*
123 Gottfried von Strassburg, *Tristan und Isolt.*

FOLKLORE AND FAIRY TALE

HAPPY-EVER-AFTER KISSES

Earlier versions of the Sleeping Beauty story were far darker than the saccharine Disney-fied familiar tale of today. In the eleventh century version, *Perceforest*, Prince Troylus, discovering the sleeping Zellandine, rapes her. Happily oblivious, the princess sleeps on. In the seventeenth-century version, *Pentamerone*, Talia splinters her finger, falls into a deep enchanted sleep and is raped by a passing king. As before, she remains oblivious until having given birth (again in her sleep) she is eventually awakened by one of her babies, who sucks out the enchanted splinter. The kiss first appeared in Charles Perrault's version of the fairy tale in 1697, *La Belle au Bois Dormant*, and she finally awoke in the Brothers Grimm's *Briar Rose* in 1812.

BEASTLY KISSES
—the type to get under your skin

Many cultures have tales of transforming kisses where a girl must kiss an array of beasts, such as bears, goats, monkeys, wolves and crocodiles. Tales such as these teach the woman that eventually she will find something to love in her unchosen one, as marriages were historically arranged matches.

In Madame de Villeneuve's version of *Beauty and the Beast*, her Beauty ponders that many girls are compelled to marry rich brutes much more brutish than her Beast, who is one in form but not in feeling or actions.

AMPHIBIOUS KISSES
—the type that leaves one cold

In *The Princess and the Frog* a spoiled princess befriends a frog whilst playing with her golden ball, which she drops into his pond. Retrieving her ball, she is forced to take him home and, despite her revulsion, must kiss him. Upon that kiss he transforms into a handsome prince. There are different versions of the tale but it is generally understood that the theme is of compliance, subservience and passivity.

NUMBING KISSES
—rendering one in a state of catatonia

Hans Christian Andersen's fairy tale *The Snow Queen* has Kai, a little boy, playing in the snow with his friend Gerda, when he is lured away by the evil Snow Queen to her palace of snow and ice. On the way there, she kisses him on the forehead—once to stop him feeling the cold, and a second time to make him forget everything. She does not kiss him again as she says it would kill him. When Gerda finally comes to his rescue, he is totally numb. As Gerda's tears fall on him, he begins to thaw and gradually revive. Once they have defeated the Snow Queen they return home....

HISTORICAL FICTION

SATIRE

François Rabelais in his fantastical satire *Gargantua and Pantagruel* ponders a welcoming papal kiss:

"O thrice and four times happy people! cried they; you are welcome, and more than double welcome! They then kneeled down before us and would have kissed our feet, but we would not suffer it, telling them that should the pope come thither in his own person, 'tis all they could do to him. No, certainly, answered they, for we have already resolved upon the matter. We would kiss his bare arse without boggling at it, and eke his two pounders; for he has a pair of them, the holy father, that he has."[124]

REDEEMING RUSSIAN KISSES
—a near perfect ending

In Dostoyevsky's *Crime and Punishment* Raskolnikov's life is a piteous existence, made ever more insufferable when he murders his unscrupulous moneylender and her half sister. Thus begins his stumbling feverish nightmare of a journey through St. Petersburg. Despite being imprisoned for the murder, it is only when he confesses to Sonja that some form of redemption seems possible. Despairing of life he asks her what he should do.

"What shall you do now?" Exclaims Sonja and her eyes flash. "Get you up go hence at once; station yourself at a crossway, kneel down and kiss the earth you have defiled, bow down thus before all the people and say to them: I have committed murder. Then God shall give you new life."

Thus he did, falling prostrate on his knees in the middle of the market place, he bowed down denouncing himself as a murderer and amidst the laughter and derision of the bystanders, he kissed the dirty ground with ecstasy and delight.

---

124 François Rabelais, *Gargantua and Pantagruel*.

GOTHIC KISSES
—soul searing and brutally romantic

Wuthering Heights by Emily Brontë (1847) conveys a sense of the Gothic to the sinister Yorkshire Moors. It features ghostly apparitions and a Byronic hero in the person of the demonic Heathcliff. Catherine Linton lies on her deathbed, condemned in love and grief by her soul mate Heathcliff, who calls her his "murderer":

> "You deserve this. You have killed yourself. Yes, you may kiss me, and cry; and wring out my kisses and tears; they'll blight you—they'll damn you. You loved me— then what right had you to leave me?… Kiss me again; and don't let me see your eyes! I forgive what you have done to me. I love my murderer."

HORROR

In Bram Stoker's iconic novel meek solicitor Jonathan Harker is held captive in Count Dracula's castle in Transylvania. Attempting to escape, he falls under the spell of three mesmerizing vampires:

> "All three had brilliant white teeth, that shone like pearls against the ruby of their voluptuous lips… I felt in my heart a wicked desire that they would kiss me with those red lips."

BITING KISSES

Sylvia Plath's account of her first meeting with Ted Hughes begins with a passionate and violent biting kiss:

> "And then he kissed me bang smash on the mouth… And when he kissed my neck I bit him long and hard on the

cheek, and when we came out of the room, blood was running down his face."

EROTICA
—French kisses of an altogether other nature…

A most sensual kiss from *Delta of Venus* by Anaïs Nin, occurs between the characters Leila, Elena and Bijou:

"The first one to move was Leila, who slid her jeweled hand under Bijou's skirts and gasped slightly with surprise at the unexpected touch of flesh where she had expected to find silky underwear. Bijou lay back and turned her mouth towards Elena, her strength tempted by the fragility of Elena, knowing for the first time what it was to feel like a man and to feel a woman's slightness bending under the weight of a mouth, the small head bent back by her heavy hands, the light hair flying about. Bijou's strong hands encircled the dainty neck with delight. She held the head like a cup between her hands to drink from the mouth long draughts of nectar breath, her tongue undulating…They lay entangled, moving very slowly. They kissed until the kissing became a torture and the body grew restless."

CONTEMPORARY FICTION

BREAKDOWN KISSES
—for a moment I lost complete control

Two years after F. Scott Fitzgerald's premature death in 1940, his old friend Edmund Wilson edited together a series of his writings entitled *The Crack-Up,* of which some originally appeared as articles, published in *Esquire* in 1936. These articles recounted his tragic breakdown; suffering from alcoholism, deeply in debt, his wife, Zelda, was committed to a mental hospital and he had given up their only child to be raised and educated by others. Bitter and thought-provoking, he writes of the kiss:

> "The kiss originated when the first male reptile licked the first female reptile, implying in a subtle, complimentary way that she was as succulent as the small reptile he had for dinner the night before."

FRENCH KISSES
—a la group

In Mary McCarthy's seminal novel *The Group* first published in 1963 there is a most vivid description of a first French kiss between Libby (one of the five central protagonists) and her Norwegian suitor. Nils has taken her in his arms, demanding she gives him her tongue. Describing his as "firm and pointed," it is with some trepidation that Libby finally succumbs to his behest.

> "Slowly and reluctantly, she raised the tip of her tongue and let it touch his; a quiver of fire darted through her…. He tried to draw hers, sucking, into his mouth, but she would not let him. A warning bell told her they had gone far enough."

INCESTUAL KISSES

The Kiss written by Kathryn Harrison describes her own incestuous relationship with her father. Having not seen each other for a decade they meet when she is a young woman of twenty. Their first kiss occurs at the airport, when he is departing. As the final boarding call is made, she kisses her father farewell and describes how her "chaste," "close lipped" familial kiss is perverted when her father "pushes his tongue deep into my mouth: wet, insistent, exploring, then withdrawn." In this instance the familial kiss is rendered sexual, creating repulsion and disgust.

DETECTIVE NOVELS

KISSES BASED ON EVIDENCE
—material witnesses sought

In the novel, which launched the detective genre, *The Moonstone* by Wilkie Collins, when heroine Rachel Verinder is kissed by her former suitor Franklin Blake, whom she suspects of stealing the priceless gem, he says:

> "I could resist it no longer—I caught her in my arms and covered her face with kisses. There was a moment when I thought the kisses were returned; a moment when it seemed as if she, too, might have forgotten. [Then] I saw merciless anger in her eyes; I saw merciless contempt on her lips."

ROMANTIC FICTION

BARBARA CARTLAND'S KISSES

Of the late grand Dame's 664 books the following eleven have kiss in the title.

Kiss for the King, A
Kiss from a Stranger, A
Kiss from the Heart, A
Kiss in Rome, A
Kiss in the Desert, A
Kiss of Life, The
Kiss of Love, A
Kiss of Paris, The
Kiss of Silk, The
Kiss of the Devil, The
Kiss the Moonlight

CHICK LIT
—perfect lightweight puckering

In Maeve Binchy's *Circle of Friends* it is Christmas in Dublin. Grafton Street is teeming, everyone out buying presents, the Christmas lights are shining, the seasonal rush is on. The air is tuneful with songs of carol singers and there on a traffic island facing St. Stephen's Green stand Jack and Benny. She is heading home to Knockglen for the holiday, and then:

> "He held her face in both hands and kissed her very softly on the lips."[125]

---

125 Maeve Binchy, *Circle of Friends*.

Poetry

POETIC KISSES

—blame it on Catullus[126]

The mesmeric power of the kiss is a staple element of the poetically inclined. It has been expressed from time immemorial in every type of poetry in every possible way. Central motifs of medieval and melodramatic nineteenth-century poetry have been the notion of the soul-mingling kiss, the death-freeing kiss (what better way to die than with your lover's kiss upon your lips) and of course the longed-for kiss. The metaphysical poets wrote of the constant turmoil where sexual and platonic love were concerned. The kiss transcended the physical and spiritual, as Nature, too, was repeatedly and metaphorically kissed.

SOUL-MINGLING KISSES

"O kiss! which souls, e'en souls, together ties
By links of love and only nature's art."
Sir Philip Sidney, *Astrophel and Stella*

---

126 Catullus's Kisses—No 7.
You ask, my Lesbia, how many of your kisses
are enough and more than enough for me.
As big a number as the Libyan grains of sand
that lie at silphium producing Cyrene
between the oracle of Sultry Jupiter
and the sacred tomb of old Battus;
Or as many stars that see the secret love affairs of men,
when the night is silent.
So many kisses are enough
to kiss you,
these kisses which neither the inquisitive are able to count
nor an evil tongue bewitch.

TO DIE WITH A KISS

"On my cold lips thy kisses thou wouldst fix,
While flowing tears with thy dear kisses mix."
Tibullus, *Elegy 1*

NATURE'S KISSES

"The gentle wind a sweet and passionate wooer
Kisses the blushing leaf and stirs up life."
Longfellow, *Autumn*

THIS PLEA EVERLASTING[127] (KISS ME)

Kiss me now
A thousand times and
Still a hundred
More and then a
Hundred and a thousand more again.[128]

To make that thousand up a million
Treble that million, and when that is done,
Let's kiss afresh, as when we first begun.[129]

And down I set the cushion
Upon the couch that she
Relaxed supine upon it
Might give her lips to me[130]

---

127 A patchwork of kiss poetry stolen from the masters (and mistresses).
128 Catullus, *Vivamus/Live with Me*.
129 Robert Herrick, *Hesperides*.
130 Sappho, *The First Kiss*.

Come gently steal my lips along
And let your lips in murmurs move;[131]

Oh might I kiss those eyes of fire
A million scarce would quench desire[132]

In tender accents, faint and low
Well pleased I hear the whispered "No!"
The whispered "No!" how little meant,
Sweet falsehood that endears consent![133]

and kisses are a better fate
than wisdom
lady, I swear by all flowers. Don't cry[134]

You may pout, and look prettily cross; but I pray,
What business so near to my lips had your cheek?[135]

I tremble when I touch thy garments rim
I clasp thy waist, I feel thy bosom's beat,
Oh, kiss me into faintness sweet and dim[136]

Give me one in your physical fashion
Give me one with your distinctive passion[137]

Kiss me; press me, till you feel
All your raptured senses reel;[138]

---

131 Sir Thomas Moore, *Teacher and Pupil*.
132 Lord Byron, *Imitated from Catullus to Ellen*.
133 Coleridge, *The Kiss*.
134 ee cummings, *since feeling is first*.
135 Horace Walpole, *Yielding to Temptation*.
136 Alexander Smith, *Kisses*.
137 Louise Labe, *Sonnet XVIII*.
138 Johannes Secundus, *Kiss XVI*.

While hard and fast I held her in my grips
My very soul came looping to my lips;[139]

We had talked long: and then a silence came[140]

And your lips clung to mine till I prayed in my bliss
They might never unclasp from that rapturous kiss[141]

We stood tranced in long embraces
Mixed with kisses sweeter, sweeter[142]

If there be an Elysium on earth
It is this, it is this[143]

For Love's sake, kiss me once again;
I long, and should not beg in vain;[144]

Let thy love in kisses rain
On my lips and eyelids pale[145]

Her response being:

Be plain in dress, and sober in your diet,
In short, my deary, kiss me! and be quiet.[146]

---

139 Allen Ramsey, *The Gentle Shepherd: Patie and Rodger*.

140 F. T. Palgrave.

141 Unknown Author, *You Kissed Me*. "The following lines were written in 1867 by a lady under twenty years of age. James Redpath, the historian, thought so much of the poem that he had an edition printed on white satin. John G. Whittier, the Quaker poet, wrote of it and its young author that she had truly mastered the secret of English verse." From the anthology *Poetic Jewels* by E. T. Roe, 1900.

142 Alfred Tennyson, *Maud Lord*.

143 Sir Thomas Moore, *Lalla Rookh*.

144 Ben Johnson, *Begging Another, On Colour of Mending the Former*.

145 Percy Bysshe Shelley, *The Indian Serenade*.

146 Lady Montague, *A Summary of Lord Lyttleton's Advice to a Lady*.

MUSIC

"Who cares to define what chemistry this is?
Who cares, with your lips on mine, how ignorant bliss is?"[147]

What note does a kiss strike, what chord is plucked, what key played? Are horn blowers and trumpeters better kissers by virtue of their more muscular mouths? If music is the food of love then might a kiss be a song, a riff, a rap, a movement, an arpeggio, a concerto? A duet or a symphony? From Mozart's musical kisses, to Madonna's kissing of Britney and Christina Aguilera, to Kiss FM, to the band KISS; presented below are a few musical notes on kissing.

A KISSING DANCE

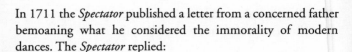

In 1711 the *Spectator* published a letter from a concerned father bemoaning what he considered the immorality of modern dances. The *Spectator* replied:

> "I must confess I am afraid that my correspondent had too much reason to be a little out of humour at the treatment of his daughter but I conclude that he would have been much more so had he seen one of those kissing dances in which Will Honey Comb assures me they are obliged to dwell almost a minute on the fair one's lips or they will be too quick for the music and dance quite out of time."[148]

---

147 "How Little We Know." Words & Music by Carolyn Leigh & Phillip Springer. Recorded by Frank Sinatra, 1956.

148 http://meta.montclair.edu/spectator/text/may1711/no67.html.

A Concert of Kisses
—sounds sublime

Adrienne Blue documents a live performance in Paris in the late 1970s where three hundred members of a concert audience volunteered to come on stage and for about ten minutes smacked kisses at each according to the conductor's baton.

Madonna's Kisses

In 2003 at the MTV Video Music Awards, Britney Spears, Christina Aguilera and Madonna performed "Like a Virgin." Britney and Madonna ended the musical number with a French kiss, followed by a second, less scandalous kiss between Madonna and Christina.

Songs to Kiss to

"A Kiss for Christmas"—Luther Vandross
"A Kiss Is a Kiss"—Rocking Chairs
"A Kiss Is Not a Contract"—Flight of the Conchords
"A Kiss to Build a Dream On"—Louis Armstrong
"A Little Kiss Each Morning"—Rudy Vallee
"A Thousand Kisses Deep"—Leonard Cohen
"Ain't Gonna Kiss Ya"—Ribbons
"Always Late with Your Kisses"—Dwight Yoakim
"An Unusual Kiss"—Melissa Etheridge
"Another First Kiss"—They Might Be Giants

"Baby Let Me Kiss You"—King Floyd

"Beach Kisses"—Dosem

"Besame Mucho (Kiss Me a Lot)"—Xavier Cugat and many others

"Blowing Kisses in the Wind"—Paula Abdul

"Butterfly Kisses"—Bob Carlisle

"Candy Kisses"—Elton Britt

"Christmas Kisses"—The Ray Anthony Orchestra and Singers

"Could I Have This Kiss"—Whitney Houston
    and Enrique Iglesias

"Cowboys & Kisses"—Anastacia

"Don't Talk, Just Kiss"—Right Said Fred

"Droppin Kisses"—DJ Sneak and Herve

"First Date, First Kiss, First Love"—Sonny James

"French Kissin' in the USA"—Debbie Harry

"Gimme a Little Kiss, Will Ya Huh?"—April Stevens

"Give Her a Great Big Kiss"—New York Dolls

"Give Him a Great Big Kiss"—Shangri-las

"Give Me Your Kisses"—Louis Armstrong

"Haul Off & Kiss Me"—Caroline Aiken

"Hold Me, Thrill Me, Kiss Me"—Mel Carter

"I Saw Mommy Kissing Santa Claus"—Brenda Lee

"I'll Kiss You"—Cyndi Lauper

"I Kissed a Girl"—Katy Perry

"I'm Gonna Dry Every Tear With a Kiss"—Johnny Grande

"In France They Kiss on Main Street"—Joni Mitchell

"It's in His Kiss (The Shoop Shoop Song)"—Betty Everett
    or Cher

"Jeannie's Last Kiss"—Bobby Bare

"Just One Last Kiss"—J. Geils

"Jus 1 Kiss"—Basement Jaxx

"The Judas Kiss"—Metallica

"Katherine Kiss Me"—Franz Ferdinand

"Kiss"—Prince

"Kiss a Pig"—Ray Stevens

"Kiss an Angel Good Morning"—Alan Jackson

"Kiss and Say Goodbye"—Kate & Anna McGarrigle

"Kiss and Say Goodbye"—The Manhattans

"Kiss and Tell"—Bryan Ferry

"Kiss and Tell"—You Me at Six

"Kiss Away"—Ronnie Dove

"Kiss from a Rose"—Seal

"Kiss in the Dark"—Pink Lady

"Kiss Kiss"—Chris Brown

"Kiss Kiss"—Holly Valance

"Kiss, Kiss, Kiss"—Jive Five

"Kiss Kiss Kiss"—Yoko Ono with Peaches

"Kiss Kiss Bang Bang"—Tough Guys Don't Cry

"Kiss Me"—Sixpence None the Richer

"Kiss Me"—New Found Glory

"Kiss Me at Midnight"—'N Sync

"Kiss Me Big"—Tennessee Ernie Ford

"Kiss Me Deadly"—Lita Ford

"Kiss Me Goodbye"—Petula Clark or Gary Puckett
    & The Union Gap

"Kiss Me in the Rain"—Barbara Streisand

"Kiss Me, Kate"—Cole Porter

"Kiss Me on the Bus"—Paul Westerberg

"Kiss Me, Sailor"—Diane Renay

"Kiss Me to the Music"—Bobby "Blue" Bland

"Kiss Me Quick"—Elvis Presley

"Kiss Me Thru the Phone"—Soulja Boy

"Kiss Me Where It Smells Funny"—Bloodhound Gang

"Kiss of Fire"—Georgia Gibbs

"Kiss of Life"—Sade

"Kiss of Life"—Friendly Fire
"Kiss Off"—Violent Femmes
"Kiss on My List"—Hall & Oates
"Kiss the Bride"—Elton John
"Kiss the Girl"—The Little Mermaid
"Kiss the Rain"—Billie Myers
"Kiss Them for Me"—Siouxsie and the Banshees
"Kiss This"—Aaron Tippin
"Kiss with a Fist"—Florence and the Machine
"Kiss You All Over"—Exile
"Kiss You Off"—Scissor Sisters
"Kiss Your Ass Goodbye"—Sheek Louch Featuring Style P
"Kiss Your Past Away"—Nine Lives
"Kisses"—Sheena Easton
"Kisses"—The Shivers
"Kisses"—Tracy Bonham
"Kisses"—Raz Ohara & The Odd Orchestra
"Kisses and Cake"—John Powell
"Kisses and Tears"—Bad Boy Blues
"Kisses Don't Lie"—Rihanna
"Kisses in the Moonlight"—George Benson
"Kisses of Fire"—Abba
"Kisses on the Wind"—Neneh Cherry
"Kisses Sweeter than Wine"—The Weavers
"Kissin' Cousins"—Elvis Presley
"Kissin' Game"—Dion
"Kissin' on the Phone"—Paul Anka
"Kissin' Time"—Bobby Rydell
"Kissing"—Bliss
"Kissing A Fool"—Michael Buble
"K.I.S.S.E.S."—Bent

"K.I.S.S.I.N.G."—Siedah Garrett
"K.I.S.S.I.N.G."—Nas
"Kissing Bandit"—Esham
"Kissing My Love"—Bill Withers
"Kissing Tree"—Billy Grammar
"Kissing You"—Des'ree
"Knock Me a Kiss"—Louis Jordan
"Last Kiss"—J. Frank Wilson and the Cavaliers or Pearl Jam
"Last Kisses"—The Nields
"Let Me Kiss Ya"—Nick Lowe
"Lets Kiss and Make Up"—Ella Fitzgerald
"Let's Just Kiss"—Harry Connick Jr.
"Let's Just Kiss and Say Goodbye"—The Manhattans
"Never Been Kissed"—Sherrie Austin
"Knock Me a Kiss"—Louis Jordan
"One Kiss for Old Times' Sake"—Ronnie Dove
"One Kiss from You"—Britney Spears
"One Kiss Too Many"—Eddy Arnold
"One Last Kiss"—Bye Bye Birdie
"Our First Kiss"—Jonathan Edwards
"Passionate Kisses"—Lucinda Williams or
    Mary Chapin Carpenter
"Prelude to a Kiss"—Duke Ellington
"Pucker Up"—Patty Larkin
"Punish Me with Kisses"—Glove
"Purple Kisses"—The Dream
"Save Your Kisses for Me"—Brotherhood of Man
"Sealed with a Kiss"—Brian Hyland or Four Bitchin' Babes
"Shut Up and Kiss Me"—Mary Chapin Carpenter
"Steal My Kisses"—Ben Harper
"Stolen Kisses"—Gene Sullivan
"Suck My Kiss"—Red Hot Chili Peppers

"Sweet Sweet Kisses"—Duke Special

"Take Your Tongue Out of My Mouth,
    I'm Kissing You Goodbye"—Ray Stevens

"That Kiss"—The Courteeners

"The Kiss"—The Cure

"The Kiss Polka"—Glenn Miller

"The Last Great Kiss of the Twentieth Century"—Darryl Purpose

"The Perfect Kiss"—Bette Midler

"Then He Kissed Me"—The Crystals

"This Kiss"—Faith Hill

"Thunder Kiss"—White Zombie

"'Til I Kissed You"—The Everly Brothers

"Toothpaste Kisses"—The Maccabees

"Venus Kissed the Moon"—Christine Lavin

"Vision of a Kiss"—B-52s

"Wasted Kisses"—Prince

"When I Kissed You"—Derringer

"What Is a Kiss?"—Do Re Mi

"When She Kisses Me"—John Gorka

"You Shouldn't Kiss Me Like This"—Toby Keith

"1000 Kisses"—Ultrabeat

"1000 Kisses"—Will Smith

BALLET KISSES

Le baiser de la fée (The Fairy's Kiss) is a ballet in one act and four scenes. Composed by Igor Stravinsky, it premiered in Paris in 1928. Based on Hans Christian Andersen's *Ice Maiden,* Stravinsky wrote it as an homage to Tchaikovsky and used several of his melodies.

Opera Kisses

The Kiss is an opera in two acts, with music by Bedřich Smetana and libretto by Eliška Krásnohorská, based on a novel by Karolina Světlá. A colorful tale involving the recently widowed Lukáš and his first love Vendulka, whose road to true love is strewn with misunderstandings, misbegotten kisses, arguments, threats, polkas, smugglers, until they eventually kiss and make up. It was premiered in Prague on November 7, 1876.

Rock Kisses

Rock and roll band KISS has recorded 37 albums over 36 years and sold over 100 million albums worldwide. Formed in New York City in December 1972, they are known for their flamboyant stage personae and elaborate live performances, which featured fire breathing, blood spitting, smoking guitars, sword swallowing and pyrotechnics. With their makeup and costumes, they adopted comic-book-style characters: The Demon (Simmons), Starchild (Stanley), Spaceman (Frehley) and Catman (Criss).

Musical Kisses

Kiss Me, Kate is a musical written and composed by Cole Porter. It is structured as a play within a play, where the interior play is a musical version of William Shakespeare's *The Taming of the Shrew*.

Kiss Me, Kate was a comeback and a personal triumph for Porter proving to be his biggest hit and the only one of his shows to run for more than one thousand performances on Broadway. It won the first Tony Award presented for Best Musical in 1949.

CLASSICAL KISSES

"My bosom urges itself
  toward him.
Ah, might I grasp
And hold him!
And kiss him,
As I would wish,
At his kisses
  I should die!"

My Peace is Gone from *Gretchen am Spinnrade* (*Gretchen at the Spinning Wheel*), a selection of text from Goethe's *Faust.* Set to music by Schubert in 1814, it was his first successful romantic or art song. Gretchen is singing at her spinning wheel while thinking of Faust. Schubert uses the piano to imitate the rhythmic repetition of the spinning wheel. At the climax of the piece, the piano stops as Gretchen becomes overly distracted by the thought of Faust's kiss, and then only hesitatingly begins again as she realizes she has forgotten to keep spinning.

SCREEN KISSES

The Edison catalogue advertised the short film *The Kiss* thus: "They get ready to kiss, begin to kiss, and kiss and kiss and kiss in a way that brings down the house every time." That one of the earliest movies ever shown commercially to the public was *The Kiss* indicates the importance of this gesture in the history of filmmaking. The screen kiss in some form or other is integral to most films.

CENSORED KISSES
—deliciously prohibited…

Incredibly, no censorship laws existed for the first forty years of filmmaking. Then in 1934 the Hays Code was introduced. These laws banned (among other things) excessive kissing, lustful kissing, lustful embraces, suggestive postures and gestures, and limited the duration of the kiss. Hitchcock famously defied the censor by interrupting the kiss scene in his film *Notorious* with a phone call. Under the code, kisses could no longer be taken lying down and an actor had to be sitting or standing. To kiss on a bed was deemed suspect and one of the kissers had to have their foot on the floor. Twin beds were the lot of married couples.

So, the intensity of the kiss began to be communicated by stylized body language including arching necks and thrusting forearms. Men were perceived as the kissers and women the receivers. Should the roles ever be reversed, women were regarded as vamps in need of punishment, or the situation rendered a comic scene.[149]

The only Hollywood ladies never to have been kissed were Mae West and Anna May Wong. It seems that Mae exuded

---

149 Famous subversions of these iron-clad rules appear in *To Have and Have Not* when Bacall initiates the kiss with Bogart; even so on exiting the room she renders all power to him when she famously says, "You know how to whistle, don't you? You just put your lips together and blow." In *Casablanca* Rick and Ilsa kiss as equals but the film ends with a famous non-kiss scene. Rick uses his black-market connection to buy two seats on the last plane out of Casablanca presumably for himself and Ilsa but changes his mind and selflessly gives it to his love rival Victor, scuppering any hope for a reunion between them.

such physicality that actual contact would have been too much. Anna May Wong's kissing scene in *The Road to Dishonour* (1929) was cut on the grounds that interracial love would offend the audience.

The Hays Code was finally abolished in 1968 and once again kisses could signify intimacy. Even so, just as early Hollywood used the kiss as an euphemism for sex, today intercut scenes of flowers touching and bees taking nectar from flowers are used in Bollywood as substitutes for showing kissing.

LEGENDARY SCREEN KISSES

The films rated as having the most romantic kisses usually include the following favorites: *Gone with the Wind, From Here to Eternity, Casablanca,* and *To Have and Have Not.* Endless lists and arguments could be proffered as to which are the most sexy, erotic, unforgettable or heartfelt. The following list contains films in which some more notorious, contentious and/ or transgressive kisses have occurred.

KISSES CAUGHT ON FILM

SHAMEFUL KISSES

In Erich Von Stroheim's *Greed* (1924) self-taught dentist McTeague (Gibson Gowland) gazes lustfully at the unconscious, anaesthetized face of his patient Trina (ZaSu Pitts). He tries to resist but succumbs to temptation and kisses her full on the mouth. Afterward, he recoils, tugs at his hair in agitation, and resumes working on his oblivious patient.

PROMISCUOUS KISSES

The 1926 film *Don Juan* was the first Vitaphone feature to include a sound track. However, it was as famous for its number of kisses. Playing a roguish Don Juan, John Barrymore kissed his two leading ladies 127 times, plus a fair few other maidens, reaching a grand total of 191 kisses.

FLESH AND THE DEVIL

The first Hollywood film to feature an openmouthed French kiss was *Flesh and the Devil* (1926–27). The kiss was enacted by Greta Garbo and John Gilbert who were lovers in real life at the time.

SHEIKY (SIC) KISSES

The legendary Rudolph Valentino starred as the titular Sheik and his impetuous son Ahmed in *The Son of the Sheik* (1926). "For once, your kisses are free!" Ahmed declares as he forces himself upon dancer Yasmin (costar Vilma Bánky) in an infamous rape scene, depicted in wide-eyed close-ups before the screen fades to black. This was Valentino's final film before his untimely death, aged 31.

Y OH Y KISSES

The first male-male kiss on the lips to appear on screen was in *Wings* (1927). Set in 1917, two young men (played by Charles "Buddy" Rogers and Richard Arlen) are in love with the same woman. They join the WWI Air Corps and their rivalry turns to comradeship. In a tragic twist of fate, David Armstrong (Arlen) is shot down by Jack Powell (Rogers). Finding his friend's dying body, Jack places a fond kiss on his lips.

DEADLY FEMME FATAL KISSES

Louise Brooks, with her famous black bob haircut, appeared as cabaret singer and femme fatale Lulu in *Pandora's Box* (1929). Caught kissing her bewitched patron Dr. Ludwig Schon (Fritz Kortner) by his fiancée, they are obliged to marry. A tragedy ensues and in the end Lulu dies during a final kiss in London's Soho with Jack the Ripper.

XX—X'S

The first on-screen female-to-female kiss occurred in *Morocco* in 1930. Marlene Dietrich was dressed in a tuxedo and top hat as performer Amy Jolly in a North African cabaret club; during one of her numbers she seductively kisses a woman in the audience full on the mouth, to the delight of the spectators.

GIRLS IN UNIFORM

Banned by U.S. censors for its depiction of lesbianism between student and teacher (Hertha Thiele and Dorothea Wieck respectively), *Girls in Uniform* (Germany, 1931) featured an all-female cast in a pioneering portrayal of lesbian love. In the offending scene all the schoolgirls knelt at the end of their dormitory beds and received a good-night kiss on the forehead from their teacher, except for Manuela who is kissed on the lips.

BABY BURLESK KISSES
(nothing cute in retrospect)

The Baby Burlesks were a series of satirical short films produced by Educational Pictures in the early 1930s. All the performers were aged between three and five years old, playing adult roles, using adult dialogue and dressed as adults from the waist up (below which they wore giant diapers with pins). Filmed in

1931–32, before the Hays Code was actively enforced, the series is considered dated and exploitative by many modern viewers and film critics because of its depictions of young children in adult and even sexualized situations.

POLLY TIX IN WASHINGTON

In this 1932 Baby Burlesk, a four-year-old Shirley Temple, in her second film role, featured as Polly Tix, a "call girl" sent by crooked officials to seduce a small-town politician, named A. Clodbuster. In the film she kisses him full on the mouth and he describes her as ravishing, to which she replies, "I'm expensive, you know."

SHAMEFUL KISSES PART II

In *Hold Your Man* (1933) a body-enveloping kiss (indicating a night of premarital sex) occurs between Jean Harlow and Clark Gable, leading to a pregnancy. The Hays Code deemed it necessary that she serve a two-year sentence in a woman's reformatory for "bad girls." Happily, redemption came, and reunited, the couple marry in the reformatory chapel.

NO MEANS YES KISSES
(aka conjugal rape)

Violent passion and conjugal rape appeared in *Gone with the Wind* (1939). Dramatically, Rhett kisses Scarlett against her will at the foot of the stairs. Ignoring her protests he carries her up to the bedroom with the oh-so seductive words, "This is one night you're not turning me out." Scarlett's contented, simpering face the following morning says everything a contemporary audience would assume about no meaning yes.

THE LONGEST KISS

The comedy film *You're in the Army Now* made in 1941 was at the time said to contain—at over three minutes—the longest kiss in film history. The lucky participants were Regis Toomey and Jane Wyman.

DEATH PACT KISSES

"There's not going to be any slip up. Nothing sloppy, nothing weak, it's got to be perfect."

Words that apply to a murderous plot to kill Barbara Stanwyck's husband in *Double Indemnity* (1944), but could equally apply to the memorable kiss she shares with Fred MacMurray to seal their pact.

DESPERATE KISSES

"Run away now quickly. It would have been nice to keep you, but I've got to be good—and keep my hands off children. Adios, adios."

Desperate for some sexual attention Blanche (Vivien Leigh) steals a kiss from a young newspaper delivery boy (Wright King) in *A Street Car Named Desire* (1951).

Adulterous Kisses

"I never knew it could be like this. Nobody ever kissed me the way you do."

"Not even one? Out of all the men you've been kissed by?"

These words shatter one of the most iconic and idyllic screen kisses when in *From Here to Eternity* (1951) Army Sergeant Milton Warden (Burt Lancaster) passionately kisses his adulterous lover Karen Holmes (Deborah Kerr) on a deserted beach.

Frigid Kisses

"I may not be Dr. Freud or a Mayo brother, or one of those French upstairs girls, but could I take another crack at it?"

Sugar Kane Kowalczyk (Marilyn Monroe) does her best to cure Joe (Tony Curtis) of his frigidity in *Some Like It Hot* (1959) and finally realizes she is succeeding when his glasses begin to steam up.

Lolita Kisses 1962

In a scene from the 1962 film *Lolita,* Humbert Humbert (James Mason) plays chess with Lolita's mother. He is winning. "You're going to take my queen!" she exclaims, to which he replies, "That is my intention." Meanwhile, Lolita, on her way to bed, brushes her cheek against his. In his next move he takes the queen and delivers the decidedly loaded line: "It had to happen sometime."

REARVIEW MIRROR KISS

Guess Who's Coming to Dinner (1967) was the first major Hollywood movie to portray interracial romance, although somewhat tellingly the only scene of physical intimacy between Dr. John Prentice (Sidney Poitier) and his fiancée, Joey Drayton (Katharine Houghton), was reflected in a cab's rearview mirror.

MONKEY BUSINESS KISSES

"Doctor, I'd like to kiss you goodbye."
"All right…but you're so damned ugly!"

In something of a visual nod to *From Here to Eternity*, Charlton Heston's stranded astronaut and scientist-ape Zira (Kim Hunter) kiss against a backdrop of crashing waves in *Planet of the Apes* (1968).

PINK KISSES

Sunday, Bloody Sunday (1971) is notable for being the first mainstream film to include a gay kiss. It portrays a romantic triangle between Glenda Jackson and Peter Finch, whose characters are both in love with the same young man, played by Murray Head.

Vendetta Kisses

Mostly associated with the Italian Mafia, the kiss of death is usually bestowed as a sign that someone is marked for death. A classic example is in *The Godfather Part II* when Al Pacino, as Don Corleone, gives his brother Fredo Corleone (John Cazale) a forceful kiss on the lips, whispering "I know it was you, Fredo. You broke my heart. You broke my heart."

Infectious Parasitic Kisses

David Cronenberg's erotic horror film *Shivers* (1975) is set in a Montreal apartment block, whose dwellers are infected by a parasite leading them on a course of sex and violence. In the final scene (which takes place in a swimming pool), Dr. Roger St. Luc (Paul Hampton) is overcome by the parasite in the form of a kiss from his infected nurse Ms. Forsythe (Lynn Lowry).

Elm St. Kisses

In the second Freddy Krueger film, *A Nightmare on Elm Street: Freddy's Revenge* (1985), Lisa Webber (Kim Myers) grabs murderous maniac Freddy Krueger (Robert Englund) and kisses him in an attempt to free her possessed boyfriend Jesse Walsh (Mark Patton). Freddy pushes her away and falls into a burning building, apparently dying. Jesse is then able to emerge from the ashes.

LAUNDERED KISSES

In 1985 *My Beautiful Launderette* broke two screen taboos with an interracial and homosexual kiss beneath a lamppost between Jonny (Daniel Day Lewis) and Omar (Gordon Warnecke).

CORPSE KISSING

In *Kissed* (1996) director Lynne Stopkewich addresses a much more scandalous taboo: Sandra Larson (Molly Parker), an assistant at a funeral home, does rather more than kiss the objects of her desire....

CUT KISSES

In *Cinema Paradiso* (1988), Salvatore Di Vita (Jacques Perrin) returns to his Sicilian hometown of Giancaldo for the funeral of the town's projectionist Alfredo (Philippe Noiret). He receives a reel of film from Alfredo's widow composed of all the censored kisses that the village priest had ordered cut from dozens of films shown by Alfredo when Salvatore was a boy. Now a famed film director, the film's final scenes show Salvatore's boyhood inspiration in a glorious montage of the forbidden kisses.

PLAGIARIZED KISSES

Cinema Paradiso, Kids in America (2005) uses a montage of famous kisses to tell a story. A teen romance featuring Gregory Smith as film-obsessed student Holden Donovan and Stephanie Sherrin as his girlfriend, it pays homage to the classic teen comedies of the '80s by re-creating numerous screen kisses. The film closes with a record-breaking six-minute-long kiss as backdrop to the credits.

NON-KISSES

One could also include some *non*-kisses in film, such as those between Bette Davis and Paul Henreid in *Now, Voyager,* when he puts two cigarettes in his mouth, lights them and hands one to her. *The Seven Year Itch* (1955) contains a more comic moment: playing "Chopsticks" at the piano with Marilyn Monroe, Tom Ewell goes to kiss her but they fall off the piano seat, leaving them flailing most unromantically on the floor. More recently in *Pretty Woman* Julia Roberts turns away from being kissed by Richard Gere, and a typical teen movie kiss moment is spoken about but deliberately missed in *Donnie Darko*.

ANIMATED KISSES

SPAGHETTI KISSES

In the 1955 animation *Lady and the Tramp,* cocker spaniel Lady and mongrel Tramp memorably have spaghetti on their first date. Sucking on opposite ends of a pasta strand the pair finally meet in the middle to kiss.

SKIN-DEEP KISSES

In the end scene of 2001's *Shrek,* Fiona the beautiful princess finally rids herself of her accursed spell when she and Shrek share "true love's first kiss"…the result being a refreshing twist on the norm where Fiona is left in ogre form—or in this case, love's true form.

TELEVISION KISSES

INTERRACIAL TV KISSES

Britain's first medical soap *Emergency—Ward 10,* one of the nation's best-loved programs, made television history in 1964 by portraying an interracial relationship between surgeon Louise

Mahler (Joan Hooley) and Dr. Giles Farmer (John White) and featuring the first ever on-screen interracial kiss. Nevertheless, the scene was softened before being broadcast as it was "a little too suggestive."

The first black-white kiss on American network television is often credited to the *Star Trek* episode "Plato's Stepchildren" aired on November 22, 1968. The kiss occurred between Captain Kirk (William Shatner) and Lieutenant Uhura (Michelle Nichols), an African American. It was the first kiss that was not racially stereotyped, in that Lieutenant Uhura was not a maid, housekeeper, or some other variant of the mammy caricature.

In this episode, the crew of the Starship *Enterprise* find themselves at the mercy of the telekinetic Platonians, a human-like race of sadistic bullies who have the dress and mannerisms of ancient Greeks. The Platonians use their powers to force Captain Kirk and Lieutenant Uhura to kiss. Fearing that the kiss might anger Southern viewers, NBC executives demanded that Shatner and Nichols lean away from the cameras and only pretend to kiss. Apparently Shatner and Nichols disobeyed.

Star Trek did in fact feature other interracial kisses: in the episode "Space Seed" (1967) a white woman falls in love with and kisses a Hispanic. On December 20, 1968, shortly after the Shatner-Nichols kiss, in the episode "Elaan of Troyius" Shatner kissed half French, half Vietnamese Nguyen Van-Nga. The fact that neither of these episodes received any particular comment would suggest that resistance was greatest to interracial kissing when it involved blacks and whites. After all, it had only been as recently as 1967 that the United States Supreme Court had ruled unconstitutional laws which forbade interracial marriage (the so-called anti-miscegenation laws).

SAME-SEX KISSES

The first kiss between two women on U.S. network television was in a 1991 episode of *L.A. Law,* when actresses Michelle Greene and Amanda Donohoe kissed. Far more controversial, however, was a kiss that appeared three years later on the family sitcom *Roseanne* (broadcast by ABC-TV on March 1, 1994). In a scene given much advance publicity by the press, guest star Mariel Hemingway kisses star of the show Roseanne Arnold on the mouth, causing Roseanne to question her own sexuality. So contentious was this episode that ABC added a viewer warning before the episode aired.

Other notable gay and lesbian kisses occurring on primetime television in the U.K. are as follows:

1987: Barry and Colin in *EastEnders* (although not much more than a peck, at the time it caused uproar in the media and questions in parliament).

1993: *Brookside*'s Beth and Margaret (as titillating as it was disapproved of).

1994: Noddy kisses pal Gary in the cinema in BBC's teen program *Byker Groove.*

2003: Todd and Nick in the U.K.'s longest-running soap opera *Coronation Street.*

2006: Men kiss in Dolce & Gabbana ad.

2008: Over two decades after the first gay kiss on prime-time U.K. television, food manufacturer Heinz is forced to scrap an ad for Deli Mayo showing a man with a New York accent, dressed like a chef, making sandwiches in a British family kitchen, kissing his husband/partner goodbye.

SPORTING KISSES

WINNING KISSES

Across all sports it is traditional for the winner to kiss the trophy. This kiss acknowledges the success of the victorious. In this it is similar to relic-kissing, which according to Catholic historian Eamon Duffy, is a sign of "the triumph of life in a world which must often have seemed dominated by suffering and death."

CURSE OF ANDY GRANATELLI'S KISS

The Andretti Curse (or the Andretti Luck) is the inexplicable bad luck suffered by the legendary Andretti racing family in their attempts to win the Indianapolis 500. On May 28, 1989, Mario Andretti finished nearly two laps ahead of his closest competitor and, upon arrival at Victory Lane, was the recipient of one of the most famous kisses in sports history—from car owner Andy Granatelli. Mario never managed to win the great race a second time. The Andretti family has had phenomenal success on the track through three generations, but neither Mario's son nor grandson have driven into Victory Lane at the Indianapolis 500.

He scores—He kisses

On scoring, soccer players will often lift their shirt to their lips and kiss it. However, in this traditionally masculine sport, kissing one another (on the lips) has often been regarded as contentious and given rise to displays of homophobia. Athletes Tony Currie and Alan Birchenall caused a soccer furor with a kiss, which turned the flamboyant long-haired soccer stars of the '70s into gay icons. Their kiss came after they inadvertently smacked into each other in a league game between Sheffield United and Leicester in April 1975. Instead of raising fists they looked each other in the eyes and kissed.[150]

Both remain with their original clubs: Currie is Sheffield United's Football in the Community officer, while Birchenall works for Leicester City's commercial department and is their match day announcer.

When soccer magazine *Four Four Two* asked Birchenall to name his worst moment in soccer, he said: "Kissing Tony Currie… Every year we have to reenact the kiss and he gets uglier by the year."[151]

Kissing Exercise

Bosnia-Herzegovina soccer coach Miroslav Ciro Blažević orders his players to kiss one another on the lips as a morale-boosting exercise (albeit unorthodox) and as a way to keep his squad

---

150 http://www.guardian.co.uk/football/2009/may/22/seven-deadly-sins-football-lust-football-first-kiss.

151 http://www.thesun.co.uk/sol/homepage/sport/football/176512/We-were-gay-icons.html#ixzz0UYTgsJLw.

unified. The coach wrote in his column on Croatian news website net.hr: "I tell them they have to kiss each other straight to the lips."[152]

HOMOPHOBIC HONDURAN KISSES

Tuesday, September 15, 2009: Honduran soccer was scandalized after a picture appeared of two players—Orlin Peralta and Brayan Beckeles—apparently kissing during the match between Vida and Deportes Savio. With homophobia widespread in Honduran soccer and their reputations at stake, the pair were forced to argue that they had actually kissed on the cheek, but that the angle of the picture had distorted this.[153]

THE KISSING BANDIT

In the U.S. throughout the 1970s and '80s, Major League Baseball games were routinely interrupted by Morganna the Kissing Bandit who ran onto the field and kissed the sports stars. Famous for her enormous breasts, she frequently referred to Dolly Parton as flat-chested compared to her. Her method of attack was to obtain a front-row seat, disguising herself beneath a large, bulky jacket. Spotting her target, she would whip off the jacket and dash onto the field wearing a T-shirt and gym shorts to plant a harmless kiss on the player's lips. On each occasion she was arrested for disorderly conduct, and her attorney once

---

152 http://www.telegraph.co.uk/news/newstopics/howaboutthat/6346472/Bosnia-Herzegovina-football-coach-orders-players-to-kiss-each-other-on-the-lips.html.

153 http://www.101greatgoals.com/picture-special-the-gay-kiss-rocking-honduran-football-orlin-peralta-brayan-beckeles/36231/.

used a "gravity defense" as explanation for her actions, claiming that her top-heaviness brought her to fall over the railings and onto the field.

AN ARGENTINE PECK

Argentine soccer fans routinely kiss on the cheek but not on the lips.

> "…So it is simple: each goal that Cani (Claudio Caniggia) makes on an assist from me, I will suck his face, right on the mouth." (*Maradona*, by Maradona with Daniel Arcucci 1995.)

Maradona did just that on July 1996 when Boca beat River 4–1 thanks to three goals by Caniggia. A miskicked penalty from Maradona hit a goal post and Caniggia scored on the rebound, a goal celebrated by the duo with a famous kiss on the lips. The moment, captured on camera and published worldwide, became known in Argentina as the *piquet*, or the peck, playing on Caniggia's nickname The Bird.[154]

BOWLING KISSES

To Kiss the Kitty or to Kiss the Jack are both bowling terminology, the former a token of great success. Shakespeare uses the term in *Cymbeline* when he has Cloten, Cymbeline's unfortunate stepson, cry: "was there ever a man had such luck! When I kissed the jack, upon an up-cast to be hit away."

---

154 Jeffrey Tobin, "A Question of Balls—The Sexual Politics of Argentine Soccer in Decomposition: Post-Disciplinary Performance" by Sue-Ellen Case, Philip Brett, and Susan Leigh Foster.

Love All—Kisses

At the 2009 U.S. Open at New York's Arthur Ashe Stadium, Rafael Nadal was taken completely unawares when, following his defeat of Gael Monfils, a fan rushed onto the court and, before security had a chance to intervene, kissed him. Rafael Nadal took the whole thing in his stride: "For me, it wasn't a problem. The guy was really nice. He said, 'I love you,' and he kissed me."[155]

The Kiss Cam

A familiar element of many stadium sports games across the U.S. is the roving Kiss Cam. Close-up images of randomly chosen participants are relayed to the huge sports stadium Jumbo-trons and the crowd cheers wildly for the two people to kiss. The original concept may have been borne of an innocent mind but unfortunately the Kiss Cam is open to abuse. Forced kisses have never sat easily on the tongue and denying same-sex kisses is even less palatable. It was reported in the *Washington Post* in July 2009 that the Washington Mystics (a professional women's basketball team) were not employing a Kiss Cam in the Verizon Center. This decision was taken as a morally protective measure to prevent children being exposed to lesbian kisses. However, same-sex kisses are tolerated as long as they are just platonic and obviously performed in jest.

---

155   Read more at: http://www.huffingtonpost.com/2009/09/09/nadal-kiss-video-man-arre_n_280252.html.

KISSING GAMES

Spin-the-Bottle

A pubescent favorite, all one requires is an empty bottle (usually stolen from one's parents' liquor cabinet) and a select number of friends sat in a circle. The designated spinner spins the bottle and whomever it points toward, the spinner must kiss on the lips; the kissee then spins the bottle, and so it goes. Variants can include forfeits, dares and more specified types of kissing or places to be kissed. A milestone in many an adolescent's life, this game can sometimes be painfully humiliating, or at other times wonderfully exhilarating.

Kiss Chase
—catch me if you can

A centuries-old game, the basic premise is that the one named "it" chases and catches their prey with a kiss. However, the desirability of the chaser can have several effects, as one might enjoy the outcome and trip-up or amend one's pace accordingly….

The game can also be played with all members of one sex being "it" and pursuing the opposite sex en masse until all have succumbed to a pucker. Usually there is no "home" or "safe place." However, in the early 1980s a variation of the game was made popular in South West London. Called Lorraine Kiss Chase after the actress Lorraine Chase, the pursued were allowed off the hook after shouting the words "Luton airport," referring to the successful Campari TV campaign of 1977 in which Chase appeared. Asked if a beauty such as herself wafted in from paradise, she first looks bemused and then answers in a harsh East End accent, "Nah, Luton airport."

DROP THE HANDKERCHIEF

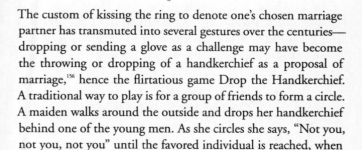

The custom of kissing the ring to denote one's chosen marriage partner has transmuted into several gestures over the centuries—dropping or sending a glove as a challenge may have become the throwing or dropping of a handkerchief as a proposal of marriage,[156] hence the flirtatious game Drop the Handkerchief. A traditional way to play is for a group of friends to form a circle. A maiden walks around the outside and drops her handkerchief behind one of the young men. As she circles she says, "Not you, not you, not you" until the favored individual is reached, when she says, "But you!"[157] However, this can be a most dangerous game—after all, Desdemona dropped her handkerchief and it cost her her life.

POST OFFICE

"Kissing her, according to Dill, was like playing post office with a dead and rotting whale: she really did need a dentist."
Truman Capote, *Answered Prayers*

---

156 http://www.traditionalmusic.co.uk/traditional-games-1/traditional-games-1%20-%20 0408.htm.
157 *Folk-lore Journal*, vii. 212; Penzance (Mrs. Mabbott).

Post Office is a kissing game traditionally played at parties by American teenagers. The group playing is divided by gender. One group goes into another space or room, called "the post office." To play, each person from the remaining group in turn visits the post office where they receive a kiss from each person in the room. Then the groups are reversed, ensuring everyone is kissed.

In the Abbott and Costello movie *Hold That Ghost* (1941), Herbie (Lou Costello) says to his paramour: "I play games, I play Post Office." When she replies: "Post Office? That's a kid's game," Herbie responds, "Not the way I play it!"

POSTMAN'S KNOCK

This is a game in which children or teens take turns to be "postman" (whose role is to go outside and knock on the door) and the door opener, who pays for the "letter" with a kiss.

SEVEN MINUTES IN HEAVEN

Another game usually played by teens. Two people are selected, either randomly or by "God" (who is nominated at the start of the game), to go into a closet or other dark corner for seven minutes. They usually kiss, but may also take things further....

NURSERY RHYMES

> Georgie Porgie pudding and pie
> Kissed the girls and made them cry:
> When the boys came out to play
> Georgie Porgie ran away

Mystery remains as to the original identity of Georgie Porgie, otherwise known as Rowley Powley. The character has been linked to historical figures including George Villiers, 1st Duke of Buckingham (1592–1628), Charles II (1630–1685) and George I (1660–1727), but there is scant evidence either way.

Of these, most believe the identity belongs to the courtier George Villiers, who led a morally colorful existence. King James I supposedly took Villiers as his lover, and Alexandre Dumas Sr. also portrayed Villiers as lover of Anne of Austria, wife of French King Louis XIII, in his novel *The Three Musketeers*.

The rhyme was first recorded by James Orchard Halliwell in the mid-nineteenth century with the lyrics "Rowley Powley" instead of "Georgie Porgie." However, the latter version was known in his childhood to George Bernard Shaw (b. 1856) and so may be at least as old.

KISS JOKES

Mabel: *That young man is very fond of kissing.*
Mater: *Mabel, who ever told you such nonsense?*
Mabel: *Why, I had it from his own lips!*

John: *What would it take to make you give me a kiss?*
Jill: *An anesthetic.*

A kiss is a noun that is used as a conjunction; it is more common than proper; it is spoken in the plural and it is applicable to all.

Q: What's an Australian kiss?
A: The same thing as a French kiss, only down under.

Q: What disease can you get from kissing birds?
A: Chirpes (It's a canareal disease, but it's tweetable)

A RIDDLE ON RECIPROCATED KISSING

A lady gave a gift which she had not
And I received her gift, which I took not:
She gave it me willingly, and yet she would not;
And I received it, albeit I could not;
If she gives it me, I force not
And if she takes it again, she cares not.
Construe what this is and tell not;
For I am fast sworn, I may not.

BY WYATT

TONGUE TWISTER

I saw Esau kissing Kate
And the fact is we all three saw;
For I saw Esau, he saw me,
And she saw I saw Esau

KISS KISS

Idioms, Sayings, Phrases

KISS-ME-QUICK,

A traditional souvenir of British seaside resorts, the "Kiss-me-Quick, Squeeze-me-Slow" hat began life as a homemade, quilted bonnet, which did not extend beyond the face. Satirist Sam Slick in his popular book *Human Nature* (1836) wrote: "She holds out with each hand a portion of her silk dress, as if she was walking a minuet, and it discloses a snow-white petticoat. Her step is short and mincing, and she wears a new bonnet called a 'kiss-me-quick, squeeze-me-slow.'"

KISSAGRAM

A greetings service for a party or celebration, in which a person is hired to come and kiss the celebrator.

KISS AND MAKE UP/MAKE FRIENDS

To be reconciled after a quarrel or disagreement.

KISS AND TELL

A journalistic term for a practice favored by the popular press in which an ordinary person sells the story of their sexual relationship (or supposed relationship) with a celebrity.

THE QUEEN OF KISS AND TELL

Known in Britain as the Queen of Kiss and Tell, twenty-five-year-old Kimberly Lee has made a career from revealing explicit details of her sexual encounters with various celebrities. Her kiss-and-tell career began at the age of eighteen when she sold a story about Robbie Williams, for which she was paid £10,000. "I'm not hurting anyone," she claims. "I never say anything bad about the people I've slept with and I never go with married men." Among her other kiss-and-tell conquests are Mike Tyson and Eminem.

KISS BEHIND THE GARDEN GATE

A rural name for a pansy.

KISS CURL

A circular curl of hair pressed flat against the forehead or cheek as worn by the singer Bill Haley. Bill Haley and his band The Comets were credited by many for being the first to really popularize rock and roll in the mid 1950s with hits such as *Rock Around The Clock* and *See Ya Later Alligator*. Blinded in one eye as a child in a bungled operation, it is said he adopted his famous kiss curl to divert attention.

KISSER

A slang term for the mouth or face.

TO KISS GOODBYE TO

To accept the loss of something.

TO KISS OFF

To dismiss or reject. To be forced to give up (something): *He can kiss off that bonus.*

To leave or disappear from notice: *got bad press by telling the reporters to kiss off.*

KISSING COUSINS

A relative close enough to be kissed on formal occasions.

KISSING GATE

A gate in a V-shaped or U-shaped enclosure, which allows only one person to pass through at a time. The person opens the gate, enters the enclosure then closes the same gate behind him to leave. If there are two people, space is so limited that one has the chance to snatch a kiss in passing.

KISS MY ARSE

A crude challenge or rejection inviting a person to perform the stated degrading act. The first known written reference is listed in the *Oxford English Dictionary* in 1705: "when you made bold with several pages of the learned Dr. Bohun without saying so much to the Dr. for his assistance as kiss my a-se" and in Fielding's 1749 novel. Tom Jones: "The Wit...lies in desiring another to kiss your a-se for having just before threatened to kick his."

KISS OF DEATH

An action or relationship that has disastrous consequences.

KISS OF LIFE

The name applied to the mouth-to-mouth method of artificial respiration.

TO KISS THE DUST

To submit abjectly; to be defeated.

TO KISS THE GUNNER'S DAUGHTER

*"I was punished, my lad—made to kiss the
wench that never speaks but when she scolds,
and that's the gunner's daughter."*
Sir Walter Scott, *Redgauntlet* (1824)

This expression, describing a punishment meted out to sailors in the Royal Navy, referred to a practice whereby the offender was tied in a bending position to a cannon, with both wrists fixed underneath so that he embraced the barrel. *A Dictionary of the Vulgar Tongue* by Francis Grose first recorded the term in 1785, and there are several variations among which are *marry the gunner's daughter* and *hug the gunner's daughter*. It is not surprising that the saying has sexual undertones given the following officer's report that boys on the HMS *Phaeton* "play on the main deck with a cane, taking turns to kiss the gunner's daughter and enact punishment. This they do sometimes with their trousers lowered."[158]

TO KISS THE MISTRESS

To make a good hit; to shoot right in to the eye of the target. In bowls the expression means to grease another bowl with your own.

TO KISS THE ROD

To submit to punishment or misfortune meekly and without murmuring.

KISS THE DICE

A custom of kissing the dice prior to tossing it in the belief it bestows good luck.

---

158   http://www.corpun.com/kiss1.htm.

FLYING KISS

The term flying kiss is used in India to describe a blown kiss.

TO KISS THE GROUND

A German expression meaning to die.

TO KISS THE CUP

An expression meaning to drink.

A KISS WITH DOTS

Is an old Judaic expression meaning an insincere kiss.

KISS

Keep It Simple Stupid or Keep It Short and Simple.

KISS TRADITIONS

THE BLARNEY STONE

In Blarney Castle on a crumbling tower
There lies a stone (above your ready reach)
Which to the lips imparts, 'tis said the power
Of facile falsehood and persuasive speech;
And hence, of one who talks in such a tone,
The peasants say he kissed the Blarney Stone![159]

---

159 C. C. Bombaugh A.M. M.D., *The Literature of Kissing*.

It is said that just one kiss of the Blarney Stone endows one with the sweet, persuasive eloquence of a native Corkonian. Built into the battlements of Blarney Castle in Cork, Ireland, the Blarney Stone is a block of bluestone said to have been presented to Cormac McCarthy, the Lord of Blarney, by Robert the Bruce in 1131. The synonymy of *blarney* with *empty flattery* apparently originates from a scathing assessment of a later Lord of Blarney by Queen Elizabeth I.

The ritual of kissing the Blarney Stone is not easily achieved. The participant must ascend to the castle's peak, then lean over backward on the parapet's edge to touch the stone. And with 400,000 visitors a year, not the least of its unpalatable features is the concentration of other people's germs, prompting Tripadvisor.com to rank the Blarney Stone recently as the most unhygienic tourist attraction in the world.[160]

KISS ME AT THE KISSING BENCH

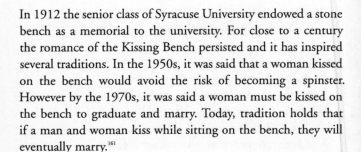

In 1912 the senior class of Syracuse University endowed a stone bench as a memorial to the university. For close to a century the romance of the Kissing Bench persisted and it has inspired several traditions. In the 1950s, it was said that a woman kissed on the bench would avoid the risk of becoming a spinster. However by the 1970s, it was said a woman must be kissed on the bench to graduate and marry. Today, tradition holds that if a man and woman kiss while sitting on the bench, they will eventually marry.[161]

---

160 http://www.telegraph.co.uk/news/newstopics/howaboutthat/5553820/Blarney-Stone-named-worlds-most-unhygienic-attraction.

161 http://sumagazine.syr.edu/summer03/alumnijournal/index.html.

Mistletoe Kisses

THE DIFFERENCE[162]

My brother is stiff—I am not stiff at all;
So when there's mistletoe hung in our hall
He manages always to miss all the kisses
While I on the contrary kiss all the misses

Kissing under the mistletoe at Christmastime is a most well-known and beloved custom. A branch of mistletoe is suspended and anyone who passes beneath the spray whether inadvertently or on purpose incurs the penalty of being kissed then and there by whomever chooses to avail themselves of the privilege.

A relic custom since the days of Druidism, the origins are believed to lie in the Norse myth of Balder, a god associated with beauty and light who was killed by a mistletoe arrow shot by his blind brother. But it was not the brother but Loki, the god of mischief who, as supplier of the arrow, was blamed. The weapon was given to the safekeeping of Balder's mother who decreed that the mistletoe arrow could never again cause harm unless it touched the ground, which is why we suspend mistletoe from the ceiling.

Historically, mistletoe was believed to promote fertility, and its leaves were said to have aphrodisiac properties. Thus mistletoe was once a part of the marriage ceremony and was placed under couples' beds for good luck. English tradition has it that a berry was plucked from the spray with every kiss and once each berry was plucked no more kisses could be granted.

---

162 C. C. Bombaugh A.M. M.D., *The Literature of Kissing.*

The Kissing Post

First stop in the Land of the Free was Ellis Island, where millions of immigrants registered in the Great Hall of the Registry Room. Those bound for Manhattan would then pass the Kissing Post, a famous wooden column, to be met by their relatives and friends. Recognized as a place for emotional reunions, it soon became known as the Kissing Post.

New Year's Kisses
—lest old acquaintance be forgot

When the bells ring out at midnight it is customary in the West to link arms and kiss to welcome in the New Year, ensuring that those affections and ties remain in the coming year. Some hold that failing to kiss denotes a year of coldness.

Valentine Kisses

Hallmark sold its first Valentine's Day card in 1913. Today, approximately 74 million romantics celebrate the holiday and 65 percent of them give Valentine's Day cards. This tradition can be traced to third-century Rome when in 270 B.C., Emperor Claudius II ordered St. Valentine to be imprisoned for refusing to recant his Christian faith. According to legend, St. Valentine befriended his jailor's blind daughter, restored her sight and wrote a farewell message signing it, "From your Valentine."

His association with romance came when a Roman celebration was combined with his martyrdom on February 14. Traditionally the Roman god Lupercus had been honored on February 15 when young women would write love notes and deposit them in a large urn to be drawn out later by young men. This was continued into the Middle Ages, when both sexes drew names from a bowl to see who their valentines would be, wearing the names on their sleeves for a week. Now, to wear your heart on your sleeve means others can easily see your feelings.

DAYS OF KISSING

If Valentine's Day wasn't excuse enough for kissing, February 5 has been chosen as International Kissing Day (except in the U.K., when it is celebrated on July 6). A relatively new event, it was instigated by the health insurance company Denplan and originally designed to promote healthy gums and teeth.

KISSES IN ESTIMATION

SOME VALUABLE KISSES

An 1899 auction to raise funds for the widows and orphans of soldiers killed in the Transvaal included a kiss donated by the aptly named Ms. Mabel Love which sold for £5.

Also reported was the case of a charity bazaar in Cincinnati in 1900 where a man who paid 7½ pennies for a kiss and found that he had kissed his own wife, "declared that he had been defrauded, kicked over several tables and had to be overpowered by two policemen."

The then record for an auctioned kiss was £800—paid by an elderly gentleman for a kiss from an American actress, the twist being that the kiss was given to his seven-year-old grandson as a birthday gift.[163]

CHARITABLE KISSES

In May 2008 Bollywood actress Shilpa Shetty raised money for charity by auctioning a number of kisses to her fans at £12,500 a kiss for the Silver Star Charity Appeal. Famous for causing Hindu organizations to riot and burn effigies of her in 2007 when Hollywood star Richard Gere kissed her on stage during an AIDS awareness program in New Delhi, she specified that this time the kiss would be on the cheek.

In May 2006 Philip Green paid £60,000 for a kiss from Kate Moss at a charity auction. Instead of receiving it himself it was planted on Jemima Khan and lasted just over sixty seconds.

Most recently in October 2009 Hollywood actress Charlize Theron took part in a live auction for the charity OneXOne in San Francisco and managed to raise $140,000 from a kiss. The bidder, a lady, climbed the stage and joined Theron in a twenty-second kiss and clench.

---

163 "Some Valuable Kisses," *Star*.

THE PRICE OF KISSES

The value of a kiss bought and paid for is one thing, but the value of stolen kisses is quite another....The question of suitable damages in the case of a young woman unwillingly kissed in 1876 prompted much discussion. The *New York Times* commented wryly that in Illinois "business and society must be dull indeed to be so whirled around on its axis by the pressure of two pairs of lips."

The lawyer for the prosecution had spoken grandiloquently of the "crimson trophy ravished from her lips," to which the defense attorney rejoined that the accused "had been in the habit of kissing her (sensation in court) and meant no harm by it on that particular occasion. He had hoped to prove—and he should have done so but for the absence of an important witness—that an engagement of marriage had existed between him and her, and that all his client could be blamed for was injudicious selection of place for his accustomed greeting." The judge ruled that the defendant should pay $10 and costs, which he paid under protest.

The *New York Times* concluded that, "When a financial value is set upon [kisses], as in this case, they generally range from five to ten dollars. [But] unwilling kisses ought to be very poor articles, and as to those that are freely given, their price is probably incalculable. They can be counted as luxuries, not always forbidden, but generally so expensive and perilous withal, that prudent folk are fain to content themselves with few, and those well chosen. There may be men who will be surprised that the Illinoisan's kiss in the street cost him but $10. They may remember kissing a woman in a church and that they have paid thousands of dollars a year for the sweet privilege ever since."[164]

---

164 "The Price of Kisses," *New York Times*.

LANA CITRON

THE COST OF A KISS

Traditionally considered taboo, the Poppy Project report of 2008 records that over one-fifth of brothels offered kissing, though at a price. Kisses ranged in cost from £10–£600; 52 percent of brothels offered kissing for only £10, 11 percent charged over £100 with the average price worked out as £42.43.

KISS STATISTICS

Online magazine getlippy.com, conducted a poll in June 2004 whereby a thousand women aged 18–25 responded to questions on kissing revealing the following statistics:[165]

> 95% of young women desired more kisses. 29% claimed not to kiss on a daily basis. 24% had gone for over a year without so much as a hint of a kiss. The average non-kissing period was three to six months for nearly 30% of women. 37% of women revealed that in their youth they had practiced the art of kissing on their hands with 11% admitting to practicing on the mirror. 25% of women admitted they were still learning!

SCRABBLE KISSES

Numerical Value: K=5 + I=1 + S=1 + S=1 = KISS=8.

---

165 PRNewswire, London, July 5.

Celebrity Kiss Crushes

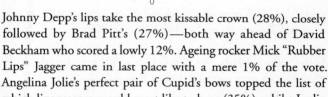

Johnny Depp's lips take the most kissable crown (28%), closely followed by Brad Pitt's (27%)—both way ahead of David Beckham who scored a lowly 12%. Ageing rocker Mick "Rubber Lips" Jagger came in last place with a mere 1% of the vote. Angelina Jolie's perfect pair of Cupid's bows topped the list of which lips women would most like to have (35%), whilst Leslie Ash's now infamous lips were bottom of the pile (1%). When it comes to the most iconic silver-screen kiss, readers opted for a modern fairy-tale classic and voted for Julia Roberts and Richard Gere in *Pretty Woman* with a third (33%) of the vote.

World Record-Breaking Kisses

Longer-Lasting Kisses

In London on Monday, July 11, 2005, James Belshaw (26) and Sophia Severin (23) broke the world record for the longest kiss by half an hour. Forbidden to sit or fall asleep, the couple could only take sustenance through a straw, and had to remain lip-locked when going to the toilet.

31:30:30 hrs James Belshaw and Sophia Severin (London) 2005
31:18:33 hrs Andrea Sarti and Anna Chen (Italy) 2004 (unconfirmed)
30:59 hrs Rich Langley and Louisa Almedovar (U.S.A.) 2001
30:45 hrs Dror Orpaz and Carmit Tsubara (Israel) 1999
29:00 hrs Mark and Roberta Griswold (U.S.A.) 1998

LONGER-LASTING KISSES
—*variations on a theme*

Forty thousand people participated in the largest group kiss in Mexico City's center on Valentine's day in 2009.

New Brighton's Alfred Wolfram kissed 8,001 people at the 1990 Minnesota Renaissance Festival in 8 hours.

The record for the longest underwater kiss lasted for 2 minutes and 18 seconds and occurred in Tokyo, Japan.

THE RULES OF COMPETITIVE KISSING

1. The kiss must be continuous and the lips must be touching at all times.
2. If the lips part, the couple are immediately disqualified.
3. Contestants must be over the age of consent in the country in which the event is being held.
4. The couple must be awake at all times.
5. The contestants must stand during the attempt and cannot be propped together by any aids, such as pillows, cushions or other people.
6. No rest breaks are allowed.
7. Couples must not leave the venue during their attempt.
8. And most romantically of all, incontinence pads or adult nappies/diapers are not allowed.[166]

And finally, should your appetite for kisses prove insatiable you may find the following recipe of use:

---

166 http://www.recordholders.org/en/records/kiss.html.

THE PERFECT KISS RECIPE

Ingredients

A willing pair of lips
True intentions (a heart full)
A smattering of sweet nothings
The whisper of bated breath
A sprinkling of sighs

Method

The success of this recipe rests on one's meticulous sourcing of ingredients; there is no room for second best. Having procured all elements, it is the easiest of procedures, merely the meeting of lip upon lip, the delicate impression of yours upon another's in a yielding moment of utter bliss.

A perfect kiss should arouse all senses. Its scent intoxicating, it should delight the tongue, tickle the lips, set one's body atingle, creating the very taste of ecstasy.

BIBLIOGRAPHY

Primary Sources
Blue, Adrienne. *On Kissing*, Indigo Edition, 1997.
Bombaugh, C. C., A.M. M.D. *The Literature of Kissing*, J. B. Lippincott & Co., 1876.
Camp, Kate. *On Kissing*, Wellington: Four Wind Press, 2002.
Carre, Yannick. *Le Baiser Sur La Bouche Au Moyen Age*, Le Leopard d'Or, 1992.
Crawley, Alfred Ernest. *Studies of Savages and Sex*, edited by Theodore Besterman. Dutton & Co., 1929.
Ellis, Havelock. *Studies in the Psychology of Sex IV: Sexual Selection in Man*, Philadelphia, 1914.
Gallup, Jr., Gordon G., Marissa A. Harrison, and Susan M. Hughes. "Sex Differences in Romantic Kissing Among College Students: An Evolutionary Perspective," *Evolutionary Psychology*, www.epjournal.net—2007. 5(3): 612–631.
Harrison, Kathryn. *The Kiss*, London: Fourth Estate, 1997.
Harvey, Karen, ed. *The Kiss in History*, Manchester University Press, 2005.
    Berry, Helen. "Lawful Kisses? Sexual Ambiguity and Platonic Friendship in England c. 1660–1720."
    Chalus, Elaine. "Kisses for Votes: The Kiss and Corruption in Eighteenth-Century English Elections."
    Das, Santanu. "Kiss me, Hardy: The Dying Kiss in the First World War Trenches."
    Davidson, Luke. "The Kiss of Life in the 18th Century: The Fate of an Ambiguous Kiss."
    Durrant, Jonathan. "The Osculum Infame: Heresy, Secular Culture and the Image of the Witches' Sabbath."
    Koslofsky, Craig. "The Kiss of Peace in the German Reformation."
    Turner, David M. "Adulterous Kisses and the Meanings of Familiarity on Early Modern Britain."
Manson, George. J. *Kissing and the Art of Osculation*, Brooklyn, N.Y.: Union Book Co., 1888.
McCarthy, Mary. *The Group*, Virago Press, 2009.
Neil, James M. A. *Kissing, Its Curious Bible Mentions*, Simpkin Marshall and Co., 1885.
Nyrop, Christopher. *The Kiss and Its History*, Sands & Co., 1901, Singing Tree Press, 1968.
Perella, Nicolas J. *The Kiss Sacred and Profane*, University of California Press, 1969.
Philips, Adam. *On Kissing, Tickling and Being Bored*, Harvard University Press, 1994.
Plath, Sylvia. *The Journals of Sylvia Plath*, New York: Ballantine, 1982.
The Iliad of Homer. Trans. by Alexander Pope, with notes by the Rev. Theodore Alois Buckley, M.A., F.S.A. and Flaxman's Designs, 1899. http://www.gutenberg.org/files/6130/6130=h.html toc16.
Tiefer, Leonore. *The Kiss—A 50th Anniversary Lecture*, The Kinsey Institute, October 24, 1998.

Secondary Sources
Aldington, Richard. *Death of a Hero*, London, 1929.
Allen, Woody. *Complete Prose*, Picador, 1997.
Amis, Martin. *London Fields*, Vintage, 1999.

Bayle, Peter. *An Historical and Critical Dictionary*. London: Hunt and Clarke, 1826.

Binchy, Maeve. *Circle of Friends*, Arrow Books Ltd., 2006.

Blakemore, Colin, and Sheila Jennett. "Kiss," *The Oxford Companion to the Body*, Oxford University Press, 2001. *Encyclopedia.com*, August 27, 2009.

Brewers Dictionary of Phrase and Fable, Millennium Edition, Cassell, 1999.

Brontë, Emily. *Wuthering Heights*, Penguin Classics, 2004.

Bufano Edge, Laura. *Locked Up: A History of the U.S. Prison System*, Twenty-First Century Books, 2007.

Bourke, Joanna. *Dismembering the Male: Men's Bodies, Britain and the Great War*, London, 1996.

Burton, Sir Richard. *Kama Sutra of Vatsyayana*, 1883.

Carver, Raymond. "Will You Please Be Quiet, Please?" Harvill, 2000.

Charles, C. H. Ph.D. *Love Letters of Great Men*, Bibliolife, 2008.

Chaucer, Geoffrey. "The Miller's Tale," *The Canterbury Tales,* revised edition, trans. Neville Coghill: Harmondsworth, 1977.

Chester Miller, John. *The First Frontier Life in Colonial America*, University Press of America, 1986.

Collins, Wilkie. *The Moonstone*, Penguin Classics, 2003.

Comfort, Alex, and Susan Quilliam. *The New Joy of Sex*, Mitchell Beazley, 2008.

Corson, Richard. *Fashions in Makeup from Ancient to Modern Times*, London: Peter Owen Ltd., 2003.

D'Enjoy, Paul. "Le baiser en Europe et en Chine," *Bulletin de la Societe d'Anthropologie, IV e Serie, VIII (1897)*, pp181–185.

Demirijian, Andrea. *Kissing*, Perrigee, 2006.

Doniger, Wendy. *Bedtrick Tales of Sex and Masquerade*, University of Chicago Press, 2005.

Dostoyevsky, Fyodor. *Crime and Punishment*, Penguin Classics, 1991.

Evans Grubbs, Judith. *Women and the Law in the Roman Empire*, Routledge, 2002.

Fitzgerald, F. Scott. *The Crack-Up*, Oxford World Classics, 2008.

Flower Smith, Kirby. *Martial: Epigrammatist & Other Essays*, John Hopkins Press, 1920.

Frijhoff, Willem. "The Kiss: Sacred and Profane," from Bremmer, Jan. N. (editor) *A Cultural History of Gesture*, Cornell University Press, 1992.

Guthke, Karl Siegfried. *The Gender of Death: A Cultural History in Art and Literature*, Cambridge University Press, 1999.

Hermann, Spencer Eisen. *W. A. Mozart*, Yale University, 2007.

Jacobs, J. "Kiss and Kissing," *The Jewish Encyclopedia*, 1925.

Junod, Henri A. *The Life of a South African Tribe*, 2nd Edition, London: Kessinger Publishing, 1927.

Lee, Carol. *Ballet in Western Culture—A History of Its Origins and Evolution*, Routledge, 2002.

Marcus Tullius Cicero (106–43 BCE), translated by Wilfred E. Major from *In Verrem (Against Verres)*.

McConville, Brigid, and John Shearlaw. *The Slanguage of Sex*, Macdonald, 1984.

Milan, Kundera. *Laughable Loves*.

Nefzawi, Sheikh. *The Perfumed Garden*.

Nin, Anaïs. *Delta of Venus*, Penguin Modern Classic, 2000.

Price, Katie. *Jordan: A Whole New World*, Century, 2006.

Proust, Marcel. *Remembrance of Things Past*, Penguin Twentieth Century Classics, 1981.

Peterkin, A. D. *The Bald Headed Hermit & The Artichoke*, Arsenel Pulp Press, 1999.

Quiroga, Horacio. *The Three Kisses*.

Rabelais, François. *Gargantua and Pantagruel*, Penguin Classics, 2006.

Reade, Charles. *Cloister and the Hearth*, Dodd Mead, September 1968.

Schaffer, Sarah. *Reading Our Lips: The History of Lipstick Regulation in Western Seats of Power*, Class of 2006, May 19, 2006.

Schott, Ben. *Schotts Almanac 2009*, Bloomsbury, 2008.

Shakespeare, William. *The Complete Works of William Shakespeare*, Octopus Books, 1983.

Stoker, Bram. *Dracula*, Penguin Popular Classics, 2007.

The Concise Oxford Dictionary, 9th Edition, Oxford: Claredon Press, 1996.

Tobin, Jeffrey. "A Question of Balls—The Sexual Politics of Argentine Soccer in Decomposition: Post-Disciplinary Performance" in *Decomposition: Post-Disciplinary Performance*, edited by Sue-Ellen Case <http://www.amazon.com/s/ref=ntt_athr_dp_sr_1?_encoding=UTF8&sort=relevancerank&search-alias=books&field-author=Sue-Ellen%20Case> , Philip Brett <http://www.amazon.com/s/ref=ntt_athr_dp_sr_2?_encoding=UTF8&sort=relevancerank&search-alias=books&field-author=Philip%20Brett> , and Susan Leigh Foster <http://www.amazon.com/s/ref=ntt_athr_dp_sr_3?_encoding=UTF8&sort=relevancerank&search-alias=books&field-author=Susan%20Leigh%20Foster> , Indiana University Press, 2000.

Townsend, Sue. *The Secret Diary of Adrian Mole 13¾*, Meuthuen, 1982.

Voltaire. *Philosophical Dictionary*, Penguin Classic, 1972.

Von Strassburg, Gottfried. *Tristan und Isolt*, edited by August Closs, Oxford: Basil Blackwell, 1947.

Waterhouse, B. *On the Principle of Vitality*, Boston, 1790.

Wilson, Glen D. *The Science of Love*, Vision, 2003.

Websites of Kiss Interest

www.oneoffkisses.com

www.charliemurphy.co.uk/kiss/

http://www.filmsite.org/

www.streetkiss.com

http://www.hersheys.com/kisses/

http://www.spymuseum.org/about/faq.php

http://www.youtube.com/watch?v=eOrKBmtC75Q

http://www.cartoonbrew.com/ideas-commentary/looney-tombs.html

www.etymonline.com

www.theindian.com/newsportal/health/kissing

Articles

Allen, Peter. "Why Swine Flu Means French Can Kiss Goodbye to Their Friendly Greeting," *Daily Mail*, September 9, 2009.

Altman, Lawrence K. "Case of HIV Transmission," *New York Times*, June 11, 1997.

Bednarsh, Etan. "The Kiss Cam Isn't for Same Sex Kisses...Except When Same Sex Kisses Are Funny," *Huffington Post*, July 27, 2009.

Bell's Weekly Messenger, April 30, 1837, and "The Law of Kissing," *Sydney Gazette and New South Wales Advertiser*, September 9, 1837.

Cockburn, Patrick. "Sealed with a Loving Kiss," *Independent*, March 23, 1997.

Devis, Arthur William. *The Death of Nelson, 21 October 1805*, National Maritime Museum, London, Greenwich Hospital Collection.

"English to Abandon Kissing," *New York Times*, January 17, 1909.

Foer, Joshua. "This Kiss of Life," *New York Times*, February 14, 2006.

Gallup, Jr., Gordon G., Marissa A. Harrison, and Susan M. Hughes. "Sex Differences in Romantic Kissing Among College Students: An Evolutionary Perspective," *Evolutionary Psychology,* www.epjournal.net, 2007. 5(3): 612–631.

Garcia, Jane. "Factoring in Beauty—A Hollywood Museum Celebrates the Artistry of a Cosmetics King," *L.A. Times*, September 22, 1991.

Grayling A. C. "It Started with a Kiss," *Guardian*, G2, July 2002.

Higgins, Andrew. "Kiss and Tell Comes to the Kremlin," *Independent*, December 6, 1992.

Highfield, Roger. "Sealed with…146 Muscles," *Telegraph*, October 17, 2006.

Hughes, Mark. "No Kissing Allowed at Warrington Station—It Blocks the Platform," *Independent*, February 17, 2009.

Kim, Gina. "Kissing: Nature's Cure-All, for Most," *Seattle Times*, February 12, 2006.

Lee, Kimberly. "The Queen of Kiss and Tell," *Independent*, August 9, 2008.

Olson, Sidney. "Dachau," *Time*, May 7, 1945.

Parker, Ian. "Our Far Flung Correspondents Swingers," *New Yorker*, July 30, 2007.

"Saved by a Kiss," *Tuapeka Times*, Vol. XXIV, Issue 1915, July 23, 1892.

Smith, Joan. "Of Mouths and Men," *Guardian*, July 6, 2000.

"Some Valuable Kisses," *Star*, Issue 7032, February 23, 1901.

"Stabbed to Death in Office Frolic," *New York Times*, February 16, 1909.

Swain, Harriet. "A Kiss and Tell Story," *Times Higher Education*, June 23, 2000.

"Sweet Kisses," *Bruce Herald*, Vol. XVIII, Issue 1833, February 25, 1887.

"Telegraph Kisses are New Fad," *Popular Science*, May 1938.

"The Danger of Osculation," *West Coast Times*, Issue 2592, January 13, 1874.

"The Galaxy Club-Room," *Galaxy*, Vol. 0016, Issue 2, pp. 280–287, August 1873.

"The Price of Kisses," *New York Times*, June 16, 1876.

Thomas, Keith. "Put Your Sweet Lips…," *New York Times*, June 11, 2009.

Titova, Irina. "Soviet Spy Who Outwitted Einstein," *St. Petersburg*, July 28, 2004.

Walter, Chip. "Affairs of the Lips," *Scientific American Mind*, February 2008.

Wilson, Giles. "Teenage Kissing: The New Sex Crime?" *BBC News* online magazine, April 30, 2004.

Woodhead, Lindy. "Stars with Scars," *Spectator*, July 22, 2006.